VIC DUNAWAY'S COMPLETE

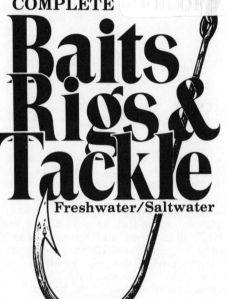

Baits Rigs & Tackle
Freshwater/Saltwater

By Vic Dunaway

Chief Illustrator
Dan Dunaway

WICKSTROM
PUBLISHERS, INCORPORATED

5901 S.W. 74 STREET, MIAMI, FLORIDA 33143

Why You Need This Book . . .

Since the introduction of its first edition nearly a decade ago, *Vic Dunaway's Complete Book of Baits, Rigs and Tackle* has become solidly entrenched as the standard reference of fishing know-how. It is the one book that covers all the key mechanics so important to fishing success, and in all fields of angling—from big-game fishing to cane-pole fishing, and all the many specialties in between. BRT, as the book is nicknamed, is as valuable to the expert as to the beginner, and its range extends from streams and lakes in every part of the country all the way to the bays and blue waters of the oceans and gulf.

The phenomenal sales success of the book's first four printings has been due as much to its simplicity and clarity as to its comprehensive coverage.

This new edition is the most all-inclusive yet, with expanded content and extensive updating to cover the important innovations in sportfishing in recent years.

For many years we have abided by this policy: If you don't agree that this book provides more useful information on more different types of angling than any you have ever seen, return it for a full refund.

It's an easy policy to stick by. With more than 200,000 copies of BRT in print, none has been returned for lack of satisfaction. So good reading, and good fishing.

—Karl Wickstrom

Publisher

NEW EXPANDED EDITION

VIC DUNAWAY'S
Complete Book of
BAITS, RIGS AND TACKLE

This new edition is dedicated to David and to Danny in memory of countless days of fun, fish and friendship; to Mari, who managed to grow up pleasant and pretty in a house with three fishermen; and to Cheryl, who somehow has lived through it all and still loves us.

TABLE OF CONTENTS

CONTENTS/continued

Chapter 1

Fishing Tackle

Spinning

Open-face spinning outfits are by far the most versatile of fishing tackle. These rigs are available in a wide array of sizes — suitable for everything from panfishing with 2-pound-test line to heavy-duty ocean trolling or surf casting with lines testing 20 or 25 pounds.

How does spinning tackle differ from so-called "conventional" tackle? Basically, the only difference is in how the reel operates, since either kind of tackle can be used over a broad range of angling applications. A spinning reel has a fixed spool which never revolves during the cast or retrieve (although it does turn when line is being pulled off against the drag). Line is retrieved by a pickup mechanism (bail and roller) which revolves around the spool as you turn the crank, thus wrapping line onto the spool. When you cast, you fold this bail out of the way, and line simply slips off the end of the spool.

By contrast, a "conventional" or revolving spool reel is designed so that the spool turns when you turn the crank. The spool also revolves in the opposite direction to surrender line on the cast.

This basic difference accounts for the rapid rise in popularity of spinning tackle following its introduction to this country shortly after World War II (it had been used here in isolated instances before then).

Because the spinning reel spool did not revolve, it immediately eliminated the beginning fisherman's chief bugaboo, the backlash. When you cast with a revolving-spool there is always the chance that the spool will get to turning faster than the lure is flying. Unless this tendency is corrected, either by light pressure of the thumb on the spool or by a mechanical device in the reel's mechanism, the over-running spool causes a bad tangle of line, called a backlash. This problem is greatly minimized in today's baitcasting reels, but it hasn't always been so.

Since a spinning reel spool does not revolve at all, there is no possibility of an over-run, hence no possibility of a backlash. After the spinning reel's introduction, a beginner could pick up a spinning outfit, and after only a minute's instruction on how to hold the line and fold back the bail, could begin to cast at once without fear of backlash. He still had to practice to achieve distance, accuracy and trajectory, but at least he was in business fast.

Let it be plainly said, however, that spinning is not free of tangles. Tangles do develop at times, but they are not caused by backlash. Spinning tangles are usually the result of twisted line or loosely wrapped line or a combination of both. They can be minimized as the angler gains experience.

Here are some other characteristics of open-face spinning tackle that set it apart from conventional gear:

The reel is mounted on the underside of the rod by means of a reel foot or mount several inches long. Naturally, the guides are on the underside of the rod shaft as well, and they extend farther out from the shaft than top-mounted guides on rods designed for revolving reels. Line leaves a spinning reel on the cast in rather wide coils and so the guides should extend far enough from the rods to prevent the line's slapping against the shaft. Also, spinning guides are of larger diameter.

This under-the-rod mounting system gives spinning tackle considerably better balance in your hands than a conventional outfit. Whether you realize it or not, some of your physical effort when casting, or simply holding, a conventional rig must be expended simply to keep the reel in upright position atop the seat. Loosen your grip and the reel will rotate instantly to a downward position.

Many spinning reels now offer one-finger operation.

Obviously, the underside mount of the spinning reel is more "natural."

A right-handed angler grips a spinning rod with his right hand by straddling the reel foot — two fingers in front of the foot and two behind it. The rod remains in his right hand throughout his fishing. He cranks with his left hand. When using a conventional outfit, the routine is to cast with the right hand, then swap hands and also crank with the right.

Can spinning completely replace conventional tackle?

Definitely not. There are certain heavy-tackle specialties where conventional gear is a must. And even in lighter, casting categories there are numerous specialties in which spinning tackle can be used, but not so efficiently as revolving-spool gear.

For instance, even the heaviest spinning outfit is not suited for line larger than 30-pound test, at most. The majority of spinning experts place the practical limit at 20-pound-test line.

Even in fresh water, a conventional outfit, in this case baitcasting tackle (also called plug tackle), is superior to spinning when you make frequent use of large topwater plugs, or when you cast with lines testing 15 pounds or more. Small freshwater spinning reels do not handle springy 15-pound line at all well. And a larger spinning reel, capable of handling stouter lines, simply is not light enough for comfortable casting over long periods. You can make do with spinning in these situations, and others, but not so satisfactorily.

11

On the other end of the scale, casting ultralight lures on lines testing less than six pounds is far easier with spinning than with baitcasting tackle, although it certainly can be done by experienced baitcasters using the modern ultralight plug reels.

SPINNING RODS

Spinning rods range from as short as 4 or 4½ feet (ultralight) to as much as 12 feet or longer for surf spinning. The two most popular lengths for all-around angling in freshwater and shallow salt water are 6½ and 7 feet. Tubular fiberglass has long been the most popular rod material because of dependability, strength and modest price, but it has largely been replaced by modern materials such as graphite and boron in the affections of serious anglers. Even in lower-cost rods aimed at casual fishermen, graphite fibers are widely used in combination with glass fibers to achieve lighter weight and more power without substantially raising cost. For that matter, many high-content graphite rods are now as low-priced as some of the better glass rods — due to higher production, more competition and ever-improving technology. Boron and boron-graphite blends are also slipping into the realm of the easily affordable.

There is no doubt that these hi-tech rods are superior in angling features to glass. They are both lighter and stronger, due to a higher modulus. This simply means that they are stiffer for their weight, and so they "load" for the cast with more stored-up energy and also have better stiffness or "backbone" for pressuring a fish.

The same qualities allow the boron and graphite rods to transmit more "feel" through the blank to the hands of the angler. He is better able to judge what his lure is doing on the retrieve; better able to feel a soft strike on a plastic worm or a gentle take with live bait.

Unfortunately, those are all theoretical observations, and though they translate from theory to practice in a great many rods and blanks made by reputable companies, there are indeed some rods labeled "graphite" or "graphite composite" that contain no more graphite than your pencil.

The best approach in rod buying these days, is to get as much advice as possible from experienced anglers and salespersons in situations where you aren't familiar with the name or reputation of the rodmaker.

One disadvantage that was a big one in graphite's early years, and is present even now though less so than before, is that the material is not as forgiving of mistreatment as fiberglass is. Accidental breakage is somewhat more likely, although the guarantees that come with "name-brand" rods help counteract this. The big companies will usually replace a broken rod under their guarantee terms so long as it hasn't obviously been used to dig post holes, or been run over by an 18-wheeler.

For all-around light spinning, choose a 6½ or 7-foot rod. The usual range of line sizes in this category is 6- to 12-pound test, and the usual range of lure or sinker weight is from about one-eighth to five-eighths of an ounce.

There never has been a standard way to define rod actions. Simply wagging a rod in the store is now less revealing than ever because there is very little "feel" to most graphite or boron rods. Nearly all factory rods, however, are marked with a range of recommended line sizes. This helps, but the individual will still have to decide for himself. For instance, one rod might be marked for 6- to 10-pound line; another for 8- to 12-pound. Let's say you're looking for a rod to use primarily with 8-pound line. You probably would choose the one marked "6-10" if you need light action for long casts with light lures in your major fishing. The one marked "8-12" will almost certainly have more backbone, and so you might choose that one if increased power seems more important to your own fishing needs than longer casts with lighter weights.

The next step up is to the intermediate category. Rods range in length from 7 to 8½ feet, but vary a great deal in action. East Coast saltwater anglers like a pretty stout tip and plenty of beef throughout, since they use their intermediate rods for tough inshore saltwater species, such as striped bass, channel bass and tarpon. And they use the same class tackle for some types of offshore fishing too. On the other hand, folks whose main fishing diet is salmon or steelhead, prefer a fast-taper rod design with quite a light tip, but plenty of "backbone" in the butt section.

Moving up again, we come to a category of 7½- to 9-foot rods, used mainly with lines testing 10 to 20 pounds. Rod action is considerably heavier than for the intermediate category—not necessarily because stouter lines are used, but because a rugged rod is needed for utmost power in fighting big fish, and because lure or terminal-rig weights may be much heavier. Spinning tackle in this class should be chosen for most saltwater offshore fishing, and some inshore fishing where large species are encountered.

A similar category is surf spinning tackle, with rods running 9 to 12 feet in length. The obvious advantage of such length is in powering out long casts in the surf. But the long rods are also useful in pier and bridge fishing, and on open party boats, particula for live-baiting.

Note that the categories defined above are only general classifications. There is considerable overlapping in areas of usefulness. And you have quite a broad leeway in making personal choices of rod length, action and line test.

Here are some quality features to look for in spinning rods:

1. Reel seats. Should be of screw-locking design and corrosion-resistant material. Graphite seats are used on many high-quality rods because it is completely inert, strong and light. Anodized aluminum reel seats are good too in those respects. Chromed brass is heavy but very strong and a suitable choice for larger saltwater spinning rods that sit most of the time in rodholders or gimbals. where you don't notice the extra weight so much.

2. Guides. The rings are the important component in guides and are available in several materials, each of which outdoes the other in one or more important characteristics. This may go against the

general grain, but the author feels that the best all-around material is stainless steel. It *can* be grooved by monofilament line, true, but it is a rare angler indeed who would ever experience grooving. Aluminum oxide ceramic, a popular and higher-priced guide material, is much harder than stainless and so will not groove. But stainless dissipates heat much faster than aluminum oxide, and heat—practically speaking—is a more real threat to monofilament than grooved guides are. Moreover, stainless guides are trimmer, thinner, less bulky and less expensive than most of the ceramic guides.

A specialty for which neither stainless steel nor aluminum oxide guides are very good choices is heavy saltwater angling for brawny and hard-running species. For this demanding work, look for guides of titanium oxide or silicon carbide. Both are good dissipators of heat and are groove-proof.

3. Wraps. The double-wrap is traditionally the most solid method of fixing guides to the rod blank. Under each guide there is a wrap of thread. The guide itself is then mounted on the underwrap, and wrapped again, usually with thread of contrasting color. Single wraps—winding the guide feet directly on the rod shaft—are found these days on many top-quality rods and are reliable because of strength provided by epoxy finishes. Double wraps may be used, of course, for sheer decoration.

4. Finish. Some low-priced rods are simply dipped in varnish. This provides a suitable finish but not a long-lasting one. Epoxy finishes, or finishes of other tough modern coatings, are widely used by the top tackle manufacturers, even on many of their lower-priced models. All quality rods will show you a gleaming coat of tough, modern material, and on the most carefully-made ones the finish is so thick and glass-smooth that the wraps underneath cannot be felt by your fingers.

Boron-graphites are generally top-of-line rods.

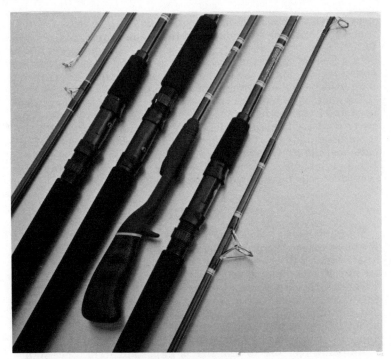
Graphite/glass composites are light and rugged.

5. Decorative wraps. Intricate decorative wraps, such as the diamond or variations, have no functional purpose, but add much to the rod's appearance and are important to many anglers. Anyway, such wraps are indicative of the rod's overall quality.

ONE-PIECE ROD OR TWO-PIECE? By and large, a two-piece rod is not significantly weaker, for most practical fishing purposes, than a one-piece. And the takedown feature, obviously, is appealing for ease of transportation. The old headache of the metal ferrule, which often corroded and involuntarily made a one-piece rod of a two-piece one, is just about gone. Butt and tip sections of most rods today fit together without a ferrule, glass-over-glass. Some have internal ferrules made of solid fiberglass. There are fishermen, though—mostly saltwater veterans—who still prefer one-piece rods, and with reasonable cause. While it's true that two-piece rods are not apt to fail at the joint in most fishing, it *could* happen in a prolonged fight with an exceptionally heavy fish at strong drag pressures. Not likely, but a slim safety factor that sways some saltwater anglers to the one-piece rod. And they're willing to put up with the inconvenience of a one-piece rod.

One more word about rod actions. You will hear the terms "fast taper" and "regular taper" often used in describing spinning rods. A fast taper rod is one in which the diameter of the blank at the butt end is quite large. The whole blank tapers with obvious abruptness from the broad butt section to the slender tip. In rods of regular taper, the variation in diameter of the blank is gradual from butt to tip.

In a fast taper rod the butt section is virtually rigid; all casting action is provided by the limber tip. A regular taper, or parabolic, rod has some action throughout its length.

The fast taper rod, as hinted earlier, is a favorite among steelhead and trout spinfishermen, and among anglers on Pacific Coast party boats, who need the delicate tip for presenting small baits.

Unfortunately, the terms fast taper or regular taper do not indicate how light or heavy a particular rod action may be. Rods of either style can be obtained in a wide range of strengths, and some fast taper rods have very stout tip sections.

SPINNING REELS

Spinning reels are functionally the same, regardless of size, and the basic reason there are different sizes is so the angler can select a reel which will accommodate a suitable quantity of the particular line size he plans to use.

Though this isn't critical for most fishing, particularly freshwater, a convenient rule of thumb to follow in choosing the proper size spinning reel for your own purposes, is to buy one which holds about 200 yards of the heaviest line you intend to use; 300 yards if you go after big, long-running fish with spinning tackle.

Matching reel size to line size is important from other standpoints too—spool diameter, overall weight of your outfit and sometimes line economy. Perhaps you could get enough 15-pound line on an ultra-light reel to serve your purposes, but line so heavy is springy and won't behave on the narrow ultra-light spool. Much better to move up to a reel with wider spool diameter. On the other side of the coin, why use 8-pound line on, say, an intermediate-size reel? You'd have to pack the spool with far more line than you ever expect to use, and the weight of the larger reel would get cumbersome when fishing.

All rules have exceptions, and the obvious one here is that saltwater anglers, who choose to work with very light line, such as 6-pound-test, will choose a much larger reel than the inland user of 6-pound—because the wider spool and larger capacity are great advantages to him with long-running fish.

Various sizes of spinning reels are needed to cover all applications. For purposes of quick review, let's divide them into the following groups, although there are many slight size variations within the groups, what with so many manufacturers these days, and so many models:

MINI-SYSTEMS—Here are the tiniest—and the newest—of spinning reels. They're little jewels with wispy rods, and have really caught the public fancy. Obviously, mini outfits turn baby fish into brawny ones, thus increasing sport and fun. But mini-systems often are used on bass and larger fish in open water, where they have the advantage of being able to present seemingly weightless lures to fish that may have become leery of larger offerings. Some of the mini reels are matched by special mounts to their own rods, but many others have traditional mounting feet and can be swapped among different little rods. Mini reels work best with lines of 1- to 4-pound test, but can be used with up to 6-pound-test.

ULTRA LIGHT—These were the smallest of all before the advent of the minis. Approximate capacity is 200 yards of 6-pound-test.

STANDARD—Light reels (the most commonly used size) with an approximate capacity of 200 yards of 10-pound line. May be used with lines in the 6- to 12-pound range, and many anglers carry an extra spool or two of different sizes.

INTERMEDIATE—A popular size for coastal fishing, and in freshwater for salmon, muskie, landlocked stripers and other large fish. Approximate capacity is 200-250 yards of 15-pound line. Frequently used with 10- or 12-pound line when extra capacity is wanted.

HEAVY—There are now a lot of big spinning reels, and you should be able to find the size you need for a hefty capacity of any line from 12- to 30-pound test.

In addition to size, you must choose for quality, especially if your fishing is of a strong and demanding type. We will look at some keys to quality in a moment, but one that stands by itself is the skirted spool.

Skirted spool reels have been around since the early days of spinning in this country, but somehow never really caught on until recent years, when Daiwa began offering skirted-spool reels of superior design and material and—of nearly equal importance in catching the public fancy—outstanding eye appeal.

This modernized offering of an old but not-too-popular reel style proceeded to revolutionize the industry. Now skirted spool reels are far and away the most popular of all, and are offered in a staggering number of models by all the major manufacturers, and many smaller ones.

The skirted spool minimizes the chance that line will creep beneath the spool and get tangled in the shaft. Skirted-spool reels also allow you to work the bail either automatically (by turning the crank) or with your hand. The spool skirt can be thumbed for extra drag pressure. And, when manufactured in one-piece, the skirted spool is far stronger than traditional spools.

Other features to check for in buying a spinning reel:

1. Ball-bearing operation. Not essential but very desirable for easy cranking and reduced wear. Probably all the higher priced reels have this feature, so you won't have to search far.

2. Construction and finish. The latest thing is graphite in major components, such as housing, mount and rotor. Graphite offers true corrosion-proof properties and is surprisingly strong. Anodized aluminum is next best. Spools, too, are being made of graphite these days. Forged aluminum, one-piece spools are the standard for top strength, however.

3. Bail. Should be constructed of heavy-gauge stainless steel wire and should click solidly into open position and snap back sharply. In skirted spool reels you may see some models with an

internal trip mechanism and others where the bail closes by the simple expedient of hitting a projection on the reel foot when the crank is turned. The latter is theoretically more trouble-free, but in practice the modern internal trips on better reels are just as dependable.

Bails on skirted-spool reels also can be closed manually; just flip the wire with your fingers. This is the way many veteran spin fishermen prefer to do it.

You also have the choice of a bail that can be opened—and the line picked up simultaneously—by one easy movement of the forefinger on your rod-gripping hand. This feature is called Auto Cast, or some similar trade name, and it amounts to a small trigger located at the line roller. Reels with this feature are self-centering; the line roller and trigger stop automatically at the top, immediately under your finger. Your extended finger, as it closes upward, first picks up the line then continues in the same stroke to depress the trigger and open the bail.

Auto Cast is considered a great convenience by many; however, some prefer the standard bail-opening system as they fear the extra gadgetry may at times foul their line.

4. Line roller. This should be made of carbide or other extra-hard material, although stainless steel is perfectly fine, so long as the roller always rolls. Be sure to check for free and easy rolling. Rollers that have a plastic sleeve or bushing may be best.

5. Drag. A positive, wide-ranging, smooth-working drag is important on every spinning reel and vital in the many situations where anglers go after fish capable of taking out gobs of light line during the tussle. This includes much saltwater fishing as well as freshwater angling for species such as salmon, steelhead and big-water trout.

The most satisfactory type of drag available on a spinning reel is the multiple-disc arrangement inside the spool. This is adjusted by turning a knob on the front of the spool. The discs (washers) are alternately of hard and soft material, the hard ones being of stainless steel and the soft ones of leather, felt or composition— or a combination of a couple of those soft materials. Teflon and leather is a common mating.

Spinning reels which wear drag-adjustment knobs at the back of the gear housing are generally smooth but not so strong or so adjustable over a broad range of tensions as are the drags already described. The back drags do use multiple washers, but they are of smaller diameter and apply their drag pressure to the shaft rather than the spool. The front drag should be chosen if you often go after big, fast-running fish that really put a drag through its paces.

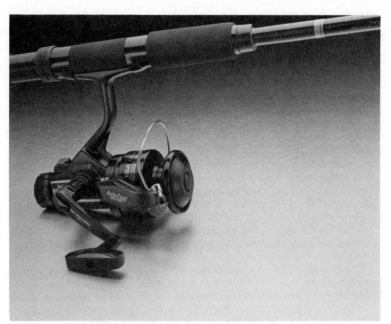

A rear-drag reel with major components of graphite.

Forged aluminum spool with drag inside is strongest type.

CLOSED-FACE SPINNING

Closed-face spinning tackle (also called push-button or spincast) is a marriage of the spinning reel and baitcasting rod. This tackle is extremely popular in all freshwater areas, but not well suited to saltwater fishing, although it is sometimes used.

The spinning reel, in this case, is of modified design and looks entirely different from an open-face reel—but a spinning reel it is, nevertheless. The spool is fixed and does not revolve during cast and retrieve.

A closed-face spinning reel is easily identified by the cone which covers the spool. There is a narrow aperture at the small end of the cone, through which the line slips. There is a large push-button at the rear of the reel, with which the angler controls his cast.

To cast, you merely push the button with your thumb, and hold the button in depressed position until the moment you wish to release the line. Then you merely lift your thumb from the button, and the cast is underway.

The reel mounts on the top side of the rod-handle in exactly the same way as you would mount a baitcasting reel. And any baitcasting rod can be used. Experience has shown, however, that reasonably light-action rods, 6 or 6½ feet long, provide the most satisfactory casting results with a closed-face reel.

As you can see, the push-button system is even easier for a beginner to use than is open-face spinning. In addition, the closed-face has been welcomed with open arms by many folks who were accustomed to the old baitcasting outfits, and who were reluctant to try open-face spinning because the operational mechanics of casting were somewhat different.

All closed-face reels are sold with spools pre-filled with line—usually 6- or 8-pound test, although some of the larger models are loaded with line as heavy as 15- or 20-pound. Naturally, you should use a stouter rod with the larger reels and heavier lines.

Counterparts of the tiny mini-systems described in the spinning section are now available in spin-cast tackle, and just as delightful to use as their spinning counterparts.

Closed-face spinning tackle is entirely adequate for just about every phase of freshwater fishing. Its only disadvantage (when compared to open-face spinning) is that the line cannot be easily controlled after the cast is underway. Therefore, the open-face rig is superior for those who wish to develop their casting accuracy to pinpoint status. However, with enough practice you can become pretty darned accurate with the closed-face too.

Saltwater fishing is another story. Here, even the larger closed-face reels are at a definite disadvantage because of limited line capacity. And closed-face reels require an extra measure of cleaning and preventive maintenance to keep them operative in a salty environment.

All closed-face reels have adjustable drags. Many are very good, but none as silk-smooth and reliable as the drags on the better open-face reels.

Modern spincast outfit

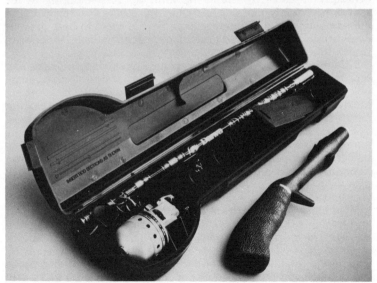

Ultra-light spincast pack outfit

BAITCASTING

The term "baitcasting" refers to a fishing system that makes use of small revolving-spool reels—most of which are fitted with level wind mechanisms to assure even spooling of the line during retrieve. You may also hear this system called "plugcasting"— a term that was originated in Florida by casters who did not like the connotation of natural bait that might be suggested by the traditional term.

During the early days of spinning's popularity boom it was widely predicted that baitcasting would fade entirely from the angling scene, but the ranks are now larger and more avid than ever, and increasing all the time.

The rejuvenation was due originally to a new generation of baitcasting reels that featured free-spool operation and adjustable drags. And now there is yet another generation of baitcasting reels in which light weight, fast spools, friction-reducing devices and modern anti-backlash aids—of which the most prominent is the magnetic cast control—have made the tackle so much more efficient, and trouble-free, that baitcasting has turned the tables and is actually stealing converts from the ranks of spin-fishermen! Actually, though, the majority of serious fishermen use both kinds of gear.

Even the reels that don't have magnetic control feature adjustable anti-backlash mechanisms that are so dependable as to make "backlash" not nearly the scareword it used to be among sometime anglers or beginners. Lightweight spools and V-shaped spools have added a measure of protection against over-runs too.

An anti-backlash device, whether magnetic or mechanical, is generally adjusted by the caster until his lure, hanging at the rodtip, will barely pull out line when the reel is free-spooled. The adjustment puts additional tension on the spool to help prevent over-running. Experienced casters, naturally, will use less tension than will a beginner.

This may surprise you: in cases where rod action, line size, and lure weight are similar for both outfits, baitcasting tackle is capable of delivering considerably longer casts than is spinning tackle. Baitcasting is also superior for delivering pinpoint casting accuracy, particularly at short range with large or heavier lures.

As in spinning, graphite and boron have taken over as the material of choice for baitcasting rods. Graphite-glass and graphite-boron composites are common too. All are much lighter than fiberglass and would be preferable for this reason alone. But they also deliver better power for both casting and fish-fighting, and transmit more sensitive feel to the angler.

Most baitcasting rods range from 5 to 7 feet in length, with 5½ and 6-foot examples being the most common. The rods typically are constructed in two pieces, those being the rod shaft and a separate reel-seat-and-grip assembly. The grip is usually a pistol-grip design, molded of rubber-like plastic or foam material. Some straight grips of the same material, or cork, are seen from time to time. The grip may be fitted to the shaft by means of a chuck, making the handle removable. Or it may simply be epoxied to the shaft.

Saltwater baitcasters often prefer a one-piece rod with a shaft that extends all the way through the butt. This is similar to the arrangement on a spinning rod except that the baitcasting reel seat will incorporate a "trigger" for the casting hand. Thru-butt design is considerably stronger for saltwater use.

A few rods with thru-butt construction but with the familiar padded pistol grip are also available.

Straight-handle saltwater rods are most commonly seen as "popping rods," which have an extended butt and are light to medium in action. They are designed to cast natural bait, or float rigs, and so the actions are usually soft. True saltwater "plug rods" have a regulation short handle, but come in a variety of actions, from very light for bonefishing to broom-handle-heavy for tarpon fishing or deep jigging. They are made mostly by small manufacturers or shops in coastal areas, although you can find a few in national-brand catalogs.

Magnetic control has nearly conquered backlash.

As with spinning rods, guides on plug rods can be of stainless steel or aluminum oxide for freshwater and light saltwater work, but should be of titanium oxide or silicon carbide for heavy saltwater applications.

Freshwater actions vary too, of course. The heaviest ones are for "worming" or live-baiting. Good, stout actions are also needed for fast crankbaiting.

In recent years, the "flipping" rod has joined the baitcasting ranks. It is longer than usual, 7 or 7½ feet on the average, with an extended butt and of stiff action. The length helps swing the lure toward target, pendulum fashion—the motion of flipping. And since most flipping is performed in heavy cover for, hopefully, big bass, muscular rods are preferred.

REELS

As previously mentioned, modern baitcasting reels feature a free-spool, star drag and anti-reverse. The free-spool is activated by pushing a button with the off hand or, in a few modern reels, by simply depressing a bar with the thumb of the gripping hand. This is the baitcasting equivalent of the Auto Cast in spinning.

In either case, the action disengages the spool from the gears so that when you cast, only the spool turns. In early reels, the gears turned and the handle spun backward on the cast.

When you begin to crank, the gears re-engage automatically.

On some free-spool reels the levelwind continues to operate during the cast, spinning back and forth across the spool rapidly as the line goes out. On others, when you push the free-spool button it also deactivates the levelwind. This is said to reduce friction, but there are anglers who claim the difference in distance is slight, at best, because of the sharp angles the line must assume to reach the stationary levelwind eye during portions of the cast.

At this writing, there is only one reel, the Daiwa Procaster Tournament, in which the two arms of the levelwind jump apart and stay at either end of the spool all during the cast. This means there is neither any back-and-forth travel of the eye, nor any sharp line angles to offer resistance to the escaping line.

It has been only in recent years, too, that a really wide array of sizes in baitcasting reels has come on the market. There are now true ultralight baitcasters, small in size and weighing as little as about six ounces. Moreover, they have the spool tolerances and spool speed to use lures weighing an eighth of an ounce, or possibly even less, and lines as light as four-pound-test. At the other end of the spectrum are reels in the Magforce series that will hold 200 and 300 yards of 12 or 14-pound-line—ample capacity even for saltwater angling of distance-minded species. And there are a number of in-between sizes.

Rods, of course, are available in sizes to match all those reels, and so now you very well may use the same approach to selecting a baitcasting outfit that has long been used in choosing spinning tackle: pick out your preferred line size and choose a reel that holds an ample capacity of that size for the fishing you plan to do.

FLY FISHING TACKLE

Almost every angler who has made a reasonable try at fly casting considers this system the ultimate in sportfishing satisfaction and enjoyment. Even more than that, it is often the best way to put meat on the table—especially when that meat is a mess of bream or trout.

In a few situations, and for certain fish, fly tackle will also produce more strikes in salt water: however, saltwater flyrodders seldom look upon their chosen sport as a *better* way to catch fish—only as a more challenging and satisfying way.

Some folks shy away from fly-casting because it seems to them an almost magical style of angling that defies their own capabilities. But really, fly-casting basics are almost as easy to learn as spinning, and with only a couple of short practice sessions virtually anyone can begin using the fly with effect for bass and bream fishing.

On the other hand, flyrodding does leave more room for improvement, refinement, and specialized abilities than any other system. If you wish, you can progress from bream and bass fishing to trout, steelhead, salmon and all sorts of specialized saltwater flyrodding.

If you are unfamiliar with even the broad concept of how fly casting works, here is a brief explanation: In other forms of casting, the weight of the lure carries out your line on the cast. In fly-fishing, all the casting weight is distributed over the working length of your *line*. Flyrod lures are, for practical purposes, weightless.

As you can now guess, fly casting requires completely different timing from spinning or baitcasting. You have to make your cast with 20 or 30 feet of line protruding from the end of the rod.

That's why spin fishermen often have a hard time learning to cast a fly. Their trouble is really not in learning how to fly cast, but

rather in *unlearning* the mechanics and timing they have been using with other types of tackle.

A beginner who has never used any kind of casting gear usually masters his fly-casting basics without the least bit of trouble.

Numerous good books on fly casting are available, and the major fly line manufacturers offer pamphlets of instruction. It is indeed possible to learn from the printed word, although much easier if you have access to personal teaching.

In selecting fly tackle, balance between rod action and line weight is of chief concern. As we will see in the following discussions, the task is not overly difficult any more, because most rods are marked with recommended line weight, and because line manufacturers have now adopted a standard nomenclature for designating weight and other characteristics of fly lines.

RODS

The majority of flyrods are made of tubular glass and range in length from 7 to 9½ feet. Split bamboo rods are still favored by a few, and still available, but the undeniable trend among avid fly fishermen nowadays is toward graphite. Some of graphite's advantages over fiberglass are mentioned in the spinning section. And, in addition to its exceptional weight-to-power ratio, fly casters like it for other reasons, among them outstanding recovery. This means that, during the casting strokes, the graphite rod straightens and becomes still much faster—to the eye, almost instantaneously. Glass and bamboo "wobble" considerably longer, and so transmit shock waves that ripple the line and reduce casting efficiency.

Early graphite fly rods had detractors among those who prefer a "slow"action rod, since all of them were very fast in action (see explanation of those terms below). But graphite now can be made into fly rods that suit anyone's taste for action.

In general, the actions of fly rods become heavier as their lengths increase. The variations to this rule-of-thumb are relatively minor until you reach 9 feet. Almost all American fly fishermen refuse to use a rod longer than 9½ feet, no matter how heavy the fishing, and the popular maximum lengths are 9 feet and 9 feet 3 inches. Therefore, you will find quite a large spread of actions in rods around 9 feet long.

Avid and experienced saltwater fly casters, for instance, own at at least two rods of different actions in the 9-foot category—a rel-

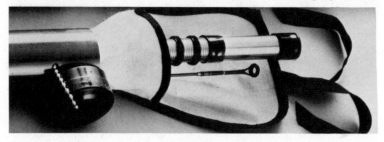

atively limber one for normal work, and a much stouter one for other sorts of more adventurous fly fishing.

When fly rod actions are described as "light," "medium" or "heavy," the reference is to the relative heaviness of the fly line needed to balance the particular rod.

Fly rods are also referred to by the *type* of action—"fast" or "slow." The *type* of action has nothing to do with line weight. A "fast" rod is one in which most of the action is in the tip section, with the butt section relatively stiff. A "slow" rod is one in which the action is distributed over the entire rod length, with considerable flex in the butt section.

The beginning fly-fisherman will find a slow-action rod more desirable.

FLY LINES

Fly lines come in a wide variety of weights (thicknesses). It is extremely important that the weight of the line be balanced to the rod for good casting performance. Fortunately, most glass rods nowadays can adequately handle more than one weight line: therefore, *minor* mismatches are not apt to be devastating, but careful line selection remains important. In most cases, factory fly rods are designated as to balancing line size.

You do not have to remember actual line weights. Manufacturers now use a standard table of numbers to denote relative weights of fly lines. Most fly lines range from No. 5 (light) to No. 11 (heavy).

Many fly lines are tapered—that is, they are thicker in some portions of their length than in others. The two most common tapers are:

1. The Double Taper. This line has a thin tip, a thicker center or "belly" section, and a thin rear portion. Designed for utmost deli-

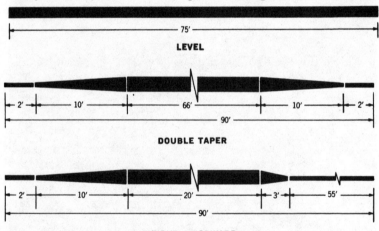

Diagrams courtesy Scientific Anglers Inc.

cacy in presenting small flies to trout, the double taper is seldom necessary in other fishing.

2. The Weight-Forward Taper (sometimes called torpedo taper or bug taper). This line has a short thin tip section which swells abruptly to a thick portion, near the tip. This thick portion is about 20 feet long. The rest of the line is of thin diameter and is referred to as the "shooting line" or "running line." Weight-forward tapers are designed for long casting with a minimum of false casting, and are especially useful in saltwater fishing, and in bass fishing with bulky poppers or streamers.

We have seen that fly lines come in different *weights* and in different *tapers*. In addition, there are fly lines that float, and those that sink. The great majority of fly lines are floaters, but sinking lines (though more difficult to pick up on the cast) are becoming more and more popular because they allow the fly caster to fish deep on occasions when fish just aren't rising.

All these variations in fly lines are neatly summed up by the aforementioned table of fly line designations. Each packaged fly line is marked with a standard set of letters and numbers which tell the buyer the three things he needs to know—what kind of taper; the relative weight; whether the line is a floater or sinker.

Some examples: DT5F (double taper, No. 5, floating); L8F (level, No. 8, floating); WF9F (weight-forward, No. 9, floating); WF10S (weight-forward, No. 10 sinking).

Only the *number* (not the letters) is important to rod balance. If your rod, for example, is suited to a No. 8 line, it will perform equally well with *any* line that bears that number—regardless of taper; regardless of whether the line floats or sinks.

Level lines are the least expensive and, for the beginner, the easiest to cast. They serve well for most freshwater fishing. Learn with a level line. You cannot take advantage of a weight-forward line anyway, until after you master the mechanics and timing of fly casting quite thoroughly. Then you may wish to discard your inexpensive level line and get a weight-forward taper (the same number, remember) in order to advance to longer casting.

FLY REELS AND BACKING LINE

Until you get into steelhead, salmon or saltwater fishing, your reel is the least important component of your fly outfit. It serves only to hold the line, so you might as well get the least expensive reel you can find, and the smallest one which will hold your line without crowding.

Most single-action reels are inexpensive. They are called single-action because they contain no gears; the spool revolves one turn for every turn of the crank.

Some people find *automatic* fly reels desirable for freshwater fishing. These have no crank at all. You wind up a spring mechanism, and then retrieve line as needed by pressing a trigger with your finger. Automatic reels are *not suitable* for saltwater fishing.

In saltwater fly fishing, you'll be after fish which make long runs—possibly much longer than the length of your fly line, which is only around 100 feet. Now your reel becomes important. It must have a larger capacity, in order to hold not only your fly line, but an attached quantity of *backing line*. It is also desirable to use a reel with an adjustable drag—and downright necessary if you go after real toughies, such as tarpon and offshore fish. However, many of the smaller, but long-running saltwater fish (including bonefish) can safely be fought from a reel with merely a strong click mechanism instead of an adjustable drag.

Large-capacity saltwater fly reels with adjustable drags are available in all price categories, starting at about $20. There are some excellent ones in the $35-$60 price range. The very best are machined from solid aluminum and cost upwards of $200. Make the choice according to your ambitions and pocketbook. Those low-priced reels are excellent values for general saltwater work, and some real monsters have been caught on them. But it pays to spend the extra cash if you plan to take on giant fish regularly.

All this fly-fishing talk—particularly about rods, lines and the balancing thereof—is bound to be confusing to the beginner. Believe it or not, this discussion has been in just about the simplest terms possible, and doesn't even qualify as a real discussion among experienced flyrodders!

But if you use the following table to pick out the type of fly fishing that appeals to you, and build your outfit as the table indicates, you can't really go wrong. Just be sure to start with a cheap *level* line. Then if you should find that a different size line works better with your rod, you're only out a couple of bucks. If your outfit balances O.K. (as it probably will), *then* get the expensive taper of your choice.

If you're acquainted with an experienced fly fisherman, by all means let him consult the table with you, and help you with your actual selection in the store.

Note that the table does not list reels. Choose your reel according to the suggestions already given, making sure it is large enough to hold whatever line or backing is called for.

Use the Uni-Knot or Nail Knot to attach backing to your fly line.

TABLE OF SUGGESTED FLY FISHING OUTFITS

Rod Length	Line Weight	Backing (Dacron)	Type of Fishing
7-7½ ft.	5-6	none	FW—Extra light
8 ft.	7-8	none	FW—Light
8½ ft.	8-9	FW—none SW—150 yds. 20-lb. test	FW—Best all-around SW—Light
9 ft.	9-10	FW—none SW—200 yds. 20-lb. test	FW—Salmon, steelhead big bass SW—Best all-around
9-9½ ft. (heavy)	11-12	200 yds. 30-lb.	SW—heavy (tarpon, etc.)
	FW—Freshwater		SW—Saltwater

IGFA OR "TOURNAMENT" TACKLE

The International Game Fish Association keeps official world records for both saltwater and freshwater gamefish in the following classes, according to line test: 2-pound, 4-pound, 8-pound, 16-pound, 20-pound, 30-pound, 50-pound, 80-pound and 130-pound. In classes from 20 up (and occasionally in some of the smaller classes) saltwater anglers use these class labels as a standard and handy reference to describe ocean fishing outfits of various size.

For instance, when someone refers to a "20-pound outfit" he does not mean an outfit weighing 20 pounds, but a rod and reel particularly well-suited to fishing with 20-pound line. Most are matched outfits designed for fishing in a specific IGFA category, and consequently this gear is often referred to as "IGFA tackle," "tournament tackle," or "class tackle."

Usually, matched outfits are of high-quality components and can be (though are not necessarily) high priced as well.

Note, however, that carefully matched tackle with a high price tag is by no means *required* by the IGFA before they will certify a world record. The IGFA doesn't care whether your catch is made with a thousand-dollar matched outfit or a $49.95 bargain-barrel rig from a discount store, so long as the line tests within the limits and IGFA specifications are met.

Still, the angler who intends to do a lot of offshore gamefishing should definitely invest in "tournament" tackle, for the simple reason that these matched outfits will do the best possible job in their particular line categories.

You can come up with some excellent matched outfits at relatively low cost—or you can shell out cash by the hundreds of dollars.

RODS

Rods designed for fishing in the various IGFA classes—the classes from 20-pound and up, anyway—are offered by several large national manufacturers and any number of regional makers or individual rod builders, usually in coastal areas of the country. These are always specified as to line class and so there is little cause for confusion in picking out the right action. You *can* shop for price, however.

Most "class" rods are fitted with a full set of roller guides and a roller top. The only real alternative to this, for offshore angling in some of the lighter line classes, is a set of super-hard ring guides, such as titanium oxide. The roller tip is retained in either case. Class rods will also generally have a gimbal-slotted butt for use in the gimbal of a fighting chair or a rod belt.

Reel seats should be of chrome-on-brass construction and pinned to the butt, as well as glued, in order to resist twisting under prolonged pressure. The best rods in the heavy categories (and sometimes in lighter ones) feature expensive reel seats machined from solid bar stock. Graphite may also be used for reel seats and gives lightness with strength in the lighter line classes.

The butt of an offshore trolling rod must be of some hard material to resist gouging and wear in a rod holder. Hardwood butts are commonly seen, and solid fiberglass butts are sometimes used. The best are butts made of heavy anodized aluminum tubing.

Traditionally, IGFA offshore rods have been made of tubular fiberglass or of solid fiberglass. The latter has often been seen even in high-priced rods from the best makers because of its unquestioned strength and the fact that these rods are generally supported by a gimbal or belt so that weight is relatively unimportant. In spinning and baitcasting, solid blanks are seen only on low-end models. They are tough but cast poorly.

As with hand-held tackle, graphite and graphite-glass composite blanks are coming to the fore in IGFA offshore tackle, and for basically the same reason—graphite's higher modulus or strength-to-weight ratio. Glass fibers combined with the graphite make these rods more "forgiving" of abuse.

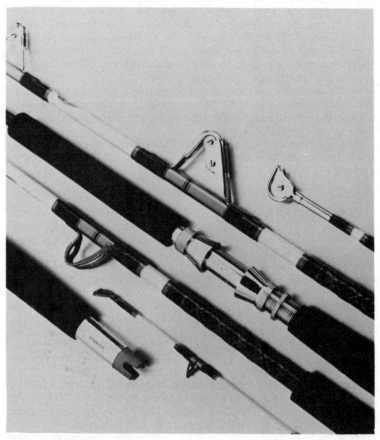

"Class" or "Tournament" Rods.

REELS

Reels used in making up matched sets for line-class fishing are divided into two broad categories: (1) Reels which have a free-spool lever and a separate star-drag mechanism. These reels are generally inexpensive, but are quite sturdy and dependable. (2) Reels which incorporate the free-spool and drag setting into a single lever. The lever in full-forward position gives maximum pre-set drag. When the lever is in full rearward position, the reel is in free spool. You have your choice of any drag in between the extreme settings, at any time.

Obviously, the single-lever reel offers a dramatic advantage over star-drag models—an advantage which is especially welcome when fighting big-game fish, such as blue marlin and bluefin tuna. Different drags are used at different stages of the battle, and with a single-lever, the angler can change settings at will.

Single-lever reels are all in the high-price category, though some brands are far more expensive than others. The lofty price-tag is not due to the sophisticated drag so much as it is to overall quality of material and workmanship. The spools, for example, are machined from solid bars of special-alloy aluminum. More metal ends up on the floor of the machine shop than in the spool.

Reels which came on the market after the IGFA started keeping records on breaking test of lines, are labelled specifically as to line test—that is, a No. 20 reel is for 20-pound line; a No. 50 for 50-pound, etc.

Brands that date back to earlier days, use a size-designation system as follows: 1/0, 2/0, 2½/0, 3/0, 4/0, 6/0, 7½/0, 9/0, 10/0, 12/0, 14/0. Not every brand of reel is supplied in all those sizes.

The larger the number, the larger the reel. And the number itself gives you a clue to the *approximate* size of line for which it is best suited, although there is considerable latitude. For instance, you might use 20-pound line on a 2/0, 2½/0 or 3/0. You might use 30-pound line on either a 3/0 or 4/0. To continue, 50-pound line on a 6/0, 7½/0 or 9/0; 80-pound on a 9/0 or 10/0; 130-pound on a 10/0, 12/0 or 14/0.

Your final choice, of course, will depend on how much line capacity you desire. It isn't a bad idea at all to spool up with considerably more line than you would normally think necessary. This is especially true when big-game fishing with heavier classes, but valid, too, in the lighter classes. You will be able to cut back line (for re-rigging, abrasion, etc.), and still be sure of having a fishable amount for a long time.

In any event, most offshore experts consider 400 yards of line a reasonable amount for 12-, 20- and 30-pound classes; 600 yards for classes heavier than 30.

BOAT TACKLE

Saltwater fishing gear designed primarily for still-fishing and trolling is called boat tackle. The term implies tackle which is not well-suited for casting.

Technically, the matched sets of tournament tackle discussed in the preceding section come under the heading of boat tackle: however, most people think of boat tackle as much more of a workhorse outfit that can be used for anything from fishing on the bottom, to occasional flings at blue water fishing.

Most boat rods are built on solid fiberglass blanks, although a few are supplied with tubular blanks. Since casting action is of no consideration at all, the solid rods are more desirable for the average fisherman. They are strong, rugged and stand up to abuse beyond the call of duty.

While boat rods are supplied in lengths as short as 5 feet, the 6 or 6½-foot models will prove the most satisfactory for all-around use. Most are low-priced, but some cost a fair amount of cash—the difference being in the amount and quality of hardware used, wraps and trim, etc.

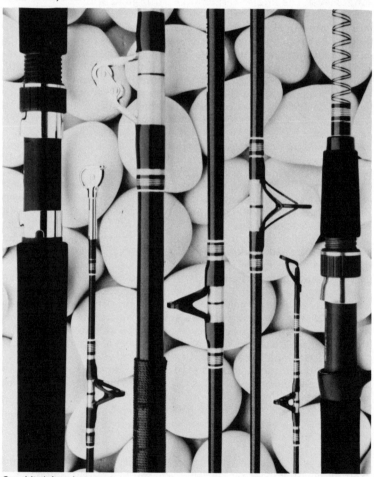

Graphite/glass boat rods.

Your own choice of a boat rod must necessarily be based on the size of line you plan to use. Most rods you'll find in the tackle store are best-suited for lines ranging between 30- and 50-pound test: however, you can find light models for 15- to 20-pound test, and some very heavy ones (often with a roller first guide and roller top) for 80- or 100-pound line, or for wire line.

Outfits built around a 40- or 50-pound line fill the bill nicely for the fellow who may fish for big groupers on one trip; for kingfish the next; for tarpon or big snook at times; and who may even go out for some bluewater trolling on occasion.

Fishermen who specialize in one kind of fishing more than others should scale their boat tackle accordingly. They might choose 30-pound line if kings and other shallow-running fish are primary targets. Or they might prefer 60- or 80-pound test if the specialty is bulldogging large bottom fish away from coral caverns.

REELS

Obviously, choosing the appropriate reel also depends primarily on the line size. As a rule, the reel should hold no less than 300 yards of line, and 400 yards would be better if much bluewater fishing is to be done—the extra amount being highly desirable in case you hook a really huge dolphin, a billfish, or some other marathon runner.

On the other hand, you might get by very well with only 200 yards if you're strictly a bottom fisherman.

It goes without saying that the reel should have a free-spool and star drag. Almost all saltwater reels do, and the few that don't are cheapies, usually plastic, that can't stand up to much pressure.

Monofilament line is by far the best for boat outfits. Therefore, it's important to make sure your reel has a metal spool. Stretchy monofilament builds pressure that will soon break a plastic spool.

Also, determine whether or not a reel has sufficiently small spool tolerance to permit the use of monofilament line. If it doesn't, your line will be constantly slipping behind the spool and jamming.

The better-known brands of metal-spool saltwater reels are suitable for monofilament. But if you have an older reel which allows the line to slip behind the spool (or if you happen to get one of the relatively few new ones that have this problem), then switch to braided line.

Monofilament is cheaper and tougher, but braided lines CAN be used for boat-rod duties.

Refer to the section on IGFA tournament tackle to get an idea of the line capacities for reels marked with the "0" system—3/0, 6/0, etc.

Some reels aren't marked by any standard system at all, but wear a hodgepodge of manufacturer's trade-names and model numbers. With those, the only way to determine capacity is to check the manufacturer's brochure or catalog.

35

SURF TACKLE

Surf comes in all degrees of wave-action, from none to booming breakers. Depending on conditions, and on how far you have to cast, you can use almost any kind of tackle to fish the surf—down to and including ultra-light spinning along much of the Gulf shore.

The term "surf tackle," however, is applied to rather heavy, long-distance, casting equipment—gear designed to toss lures or sinkers weighing several ounces far out over the big breakers.

Surf rods are characterized by stout tips and very long butts. Overall length may range from as little as 8 feet to as much as 14 feet, sometimes longer than that.

The stoutest of all surf outfits are those used for tossing out bottom rigs with heavy pyramid sinkers—mainly in quest of big redfish (channel bass), or big black drum. It takes a lot of rod to handle five or six ounces of sinker, and so the tips of these heavy-duty sticks are as big around as your thumb.

Though longer rods are available, many surf specialists agree that 10- or 11-footers are ideal for this work.

Surf reels are similar in appearance to other free-spool, star-drag saltwater reels. But they generally have a wider spool, and design

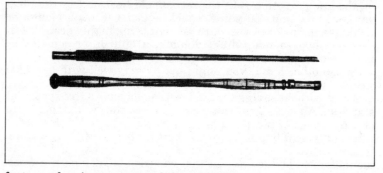

features that improve castability. They may be called "squidding reels," or simply "ocean casting reels," as well as surf reels.

The line also is generally called "squidding" line, and is made of braided nylon. Tests range from 18 to 54 pounds, with the most popular sizes being 27 and 36 pounds. The odd sizes of pound-test designation are holdovers from the days of linen (Cuttyhunk) lines.

The true surf-fishing specialist owns at least two outfits, and probably more than that. He will have one of the "broomstick" rods already described, and most likely use it with 36-pound-test line for casting heavy bottom rigs or the biggest metal squids.

He also will have a lighter outfit—a more flexible and perhaps longer rod, which he will use with smaller line to throw artificial lures and bottom rigs weighing up to 2 or 3 ounces.

This second outfit might be a conventional surf rig, with 18- or 27-pound squidding line; or it might be a surf-spinning outfit with 20- or 25-pound-test monofilament.

See the section on Spinning Tackle for recommendations as to surf-spinning gear.

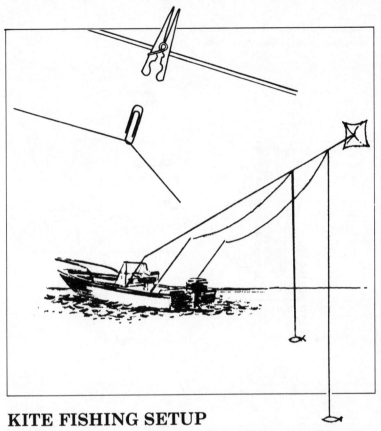

KITE FISHING SETUP

Kite fishing is widely practiced in Florida waters nowadays, and has spread to many other areas. Its basic use is to fish live baits well away from an anchored or drifting boat, although it can be used for trolling with either live or rigged baits.

The first illustration shows the arrangement of kite, kite line and fishing lines. The second drawing shows how the fishing line is attached to the kite line.

As you can see, one or two clothespins are attached to the kite line, much in the manner of an outrigger arrangement. Your line attaches to the clothespin, and then the kite is allowed to soar to the desired distance from the boat, taking your line with it.

Obviously, you must not attach your line *directly* to the clothespin. You must use some sort of a loop, through which your line can run freely, so the desired amount of line can be let out. It is this *loop* which you snap to the pin.

Items most commonly used as a free-running "loop" are an extra swivel, or a common paper clip. If the swivel is used, thread one eye of it through your line *before* tying on your leader. The other eye of the swivel attaches to the clothespin. The paper clip is handier because you can snap it on and off your line without disturbing the leader.

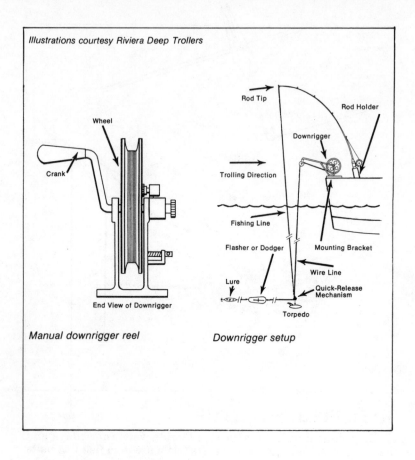

Manual downrigger reel

Downrigger setup

DOWNRIGGERS

By far the most efficient tool ever devised for deep trolling is the downrigger, sometimes called the underwater outrigger. It is the only deep-fishing system which allows the angler a controllable variation in depth, plus the ability to keep his bait or lure faithfully at that selected depth.

Homemade versions of the downrigger have been in scattered use over many waters of the world for many years, but not until the introduction of Pacific salmon to the Great Lakes in the mid-1960s did downrigger fishing come into wide use, or did manufactured downrigger setups reach a high degree of dependability, portability and sophistication. Various models are now offered by several manufacturers, some of them motorized.

Great Lakes anglers seeking coho and chinook salmon remain the chief users of downriggers, but the system has expanded rapidly in recent years and now is commonly seen in saltwater fishing on all coasts, and in scattered deep-lake situations for many species, including lake trout and walleye. In the Great Lakes, both coho and chinook salmon can be caught near the surface in spring and fall, but throughout the summer can only be taken deep. Coho prefer a water temperature of around 53 degrees fahrenheit, and this may at times be 200 feet down.

But even at much shallower depths—whether for salmon or strictly saltwater species—the downrigger still excels simply because your depth may be chosen and maintained, be it 20 feet or 200.

Downriggers are large reels, spooled with wire cable. To the end of the cable is snapped a heavy weight, which is lowered from the spool via an arm-and-pulley arrangement. On the weight is a release device to which your fishing line is clipped.

The weight carries your line and lure to the desired depth, whereupon the downrigger spool is locked. A digital counter on the downrigger spells out the depth for you. When a fish strikes, the fishing line is pulled from its pin, and you fight the fish unencumbered by the heavy sinkers or planing devices necessary in other types of deep-fishing.

Once a hookup is achieved, the downrigger weight should be cranked up out of the way. As mentioned, some of the more expensive models are motorized to do the job in push-button fashion. Most, however, have hand cranks. Due to the large diameter of the spool, hand-cranking is not too exhausting a job. Two or more downriggers can easily be used on one boat. Once a mounting bracket is installed on gunwale or transom, the downrigger can be set up and removed at will.

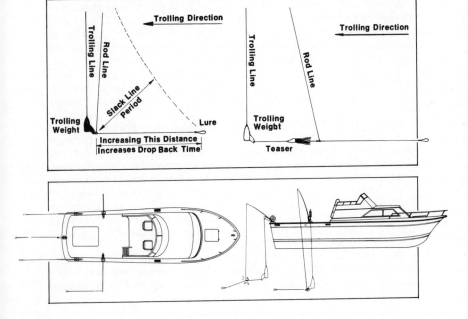

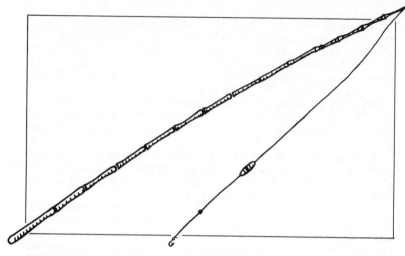

RIGGING THE CANE POLE

Cane poles not only are maintaining their popularity, but are actually increasing in use as the years go by. Kids use them, of course, but so do a lot of grownups. Nobody can dispute the effectiveness of a pole for producing good strings of bream, perch, catfish and many other species.

Plenty of bass are caught on cane poles, too—sometimes by mistake, but often by design. And one particular type of cane pole fishing—called jigger-fishing or skittering—may be the best method of all for consistently producing really big bass.

Advances in poles have managed to keep pretty well abreast of advances in rods and reels. You can still buy the old-fashioned cane pole just about everywhere, and in a great variety of lengths and strengths. You can also buy two, three and four-piece disjointed poles with friction ferrules or screw-type ferrules.

Then, of course, there are the telescoping fiberglass poles, which cost a few bucks, but which stow and transport easily, and which generally outlast far more than their equal money value in cane poles.

As a rule of thumb, you should use as long a pole as you can comfortably handle. Twelve and 14-footers are about right for most people in most situations, but a lot of fishermen like 16 and 18-footers. Of course, you might use the long poles for lake fishing, but have shorter ones, too, for fishing in tight creeks or bushy spots.

For bream, perch or crappie fishing, use monofilament line of 10 to 15-pound test. First tie the line snugly around the pole about two feet down from the tip—say at around the third or fourth joint of bamboo. Then spiral the line upward around the tip and tie it again at the very end of the pole.

Why the double tie? Because it is not at all unusual for a cane pole to break at the tip—especially if you're surprised by a husky bass or catfish. Should the tip break, you're protected by the second tie, and may not lose your rig or your fish.

Your line should be about the same length as the pole, or perhaps a couple feet longer. Lines longer than that are difficult to handle.

If you plan to bass-fish with live bait, or go catfishing, you rig your pole in the same way, but with heavier line (and usually a heavier pole too).

Although the great majority of pole fishermen use corks or floats to signal a bite, some of the very best ones use no cork at all. They can better explore different depths, and are always sure of getting their bait to the bottom when they want to, without having to test and adjust corks. Then too, they say a biting fish is never spooked away by the resistance of a cork.

How do you tell a bite, when there's no float on your line? Try it. You'll be surprised how well you can feel even the lightest tap if you concentrate. Also, if your bait is resting on bottom, the movement of your line through the water indicates a bite.

THE BUSH LINE

Another pet of catfishermen is the bushline. These lines are normally put out in number along the bank of a river before dark, then checked either next morning or once or twice during the night.

The line is tied to a sturdy but springy branch. The hook is baited with cut bait, liver, etc. (see Catfish Baits in another chapter). These lines are fished shallow—often just at or under the surface. It is not necessary, *at night,* to fish catfish on the bottom.

When a catfish is hooked on a bush line, the springy limb "plays" the fish and prevents him from pulling the hook.

As with trot lines, be sure to check on the legality of bush lines in particular areas. There may be restrictions.

41

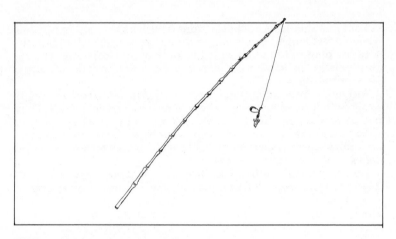

THE JIGGER POLE

"Jigger fishing" is probably the oldest known method of taking bass on an artificial lure—and still one of the best. It doesn't appeal to every angler, but it always has had a staunch corps of followers. And anyone who develops a knack for jigger fishing can produce bass like magic, particularly at night.

(The system is also referred to as "skittering," "doodle-socking," and by various other local names.)

Jigger fishing was described by famed naturalist William Bartram in his writings on Florida during the period 1773-1778—and apparently it was long-established even then!

Jigger fishermen use a very strong cane pole, usually 12 or 14 feet long, and a very short line from two to three feet long. The line should test at least 40 pounds.

Tie the line first about two or three joints back from the tip of the pole. Spiral the line around the pole to the tip, and tie again.

The jigger lure is almost always home made, but generally features a very large spinner and a hefty treble hook dressed with bucktail or feathers. Some anglers use strips of flannel, pork chunks, even artificial eels. Whatever type of lure is selected, it seems to make little difference to the bass.

Far more important is a deft and patient touch in zig-zagging the lure across the surface with as much commotion as possible.

The style is usually practiced by two men—one sitting in the bow of the boat and skittering the lure steadily along the shoreline or around weeds; the other sitting in the stern and paddling slowly along.

You can also jigger-fish by walking along a shoreline or wading.

When the bass hits, you don't lift the pole, as you would when fishing for bream. You first jerk the pole towards you to set the hook, and then you sort of handline the pole toward you until the fish comes in reach of your net.

Not sporting, say some people, but nobody can deny that it's exciting—and productive.

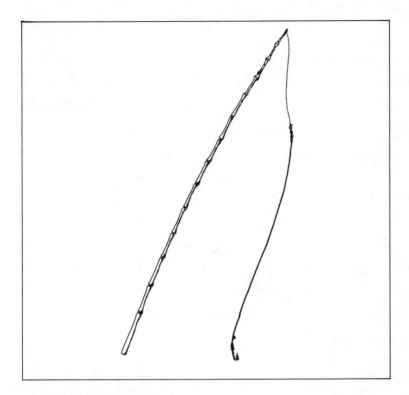

CALCUTTA POLE

Some sportsmen sneer at the Calcutta pole as "meat fisher-man's" tool. So it may be, but the fact remains that a lot of specialists still use it for such heavy-duty jobs as catching snook from bridges or jewfish from around mangrove cutbanks. The whole idea is to use something stout enough so you can simply overpower big fish in situations where rod-and-reel normally leads to a quick cutoff.

It goes without saying that you need muscle and daring to tackle the big ones in this manner.

Use only heavy braided line (130-pound-test or heavier) for attaching to the Calcutta. Tie the line tightly around your pole three or four joints back from the tip, then spiral the line around the pole several times until you reach the top. Take two or three wraps around the tip, and tie the line again at least twice.

You should have a foot or two of braided line dangling from the tip. To the braided line, tie a large, heavy-duty swivel. The rest of your line is made up of stout wire leader, at least No. 9, and the overall length should be just about the length of the pole.

Wrap the wire to both swivel and hook with the Haywire Twist.

Only heavy-duty forged hooks should be used with this rig, or the hook is apt to straighten under the heavy pressure expected.

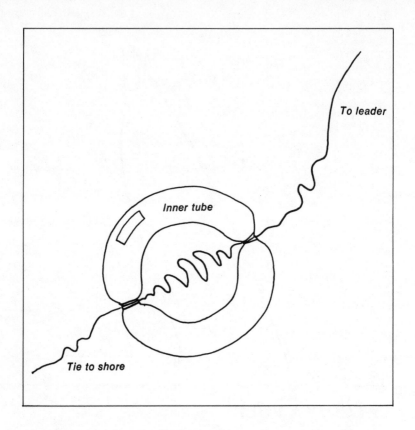

To leader

Inner tube

Tie to shore

SET LINE FOR JEWFISH AND SHARK

Many people like to leave out a heavy set-line on a dock, bridge or shore in hopes of catching some monster, such as a shark, jewfish, sawfish or giant ray. This line is left unattended, while the people involved go about normal fishing, or other activities. They check the line from time to time, and perhaps even rig up a cowbell to it to act as an alarm.

The "line" of course is usually rope—quarter-inch nylon is often chosen. You need an extra-big swivel in order to tie the rope to it. Leader wire should be heavy cable, No. 15 single-strand wire, or a shark hook and chain leader.

The key to this rig is an old (but not rotten) automobile tire inner-tube. This is tied to the rope, pretty close to the point where you anchor the rope firmly to a piling or tree. Tie your line to one side of the inner tube, allow some slack, then tie to the other side of the tube, directly opposite the first tie.

Once the monster is hooked, the stretch of the tube "plays" him. Without the tube to absorb shock, your monster might break the rope or pull loose from the hook. Use only the stoutest hooks obtainable.

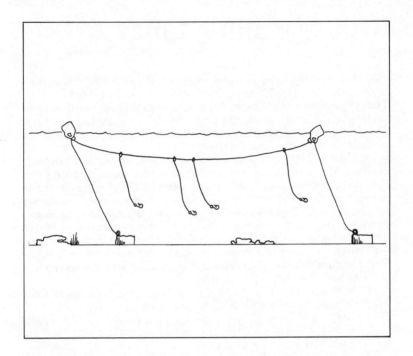

THE TROT LINE

The trot line, used for taking catfish, is merely a long and stout line of any desired length, with dropper lines coming off it at regularly spaced intervals. Each dropper line is rigged with a hook, and usually a sinker. To avoid buying sinkers in quantity, the trotliner may merely weight his lines with old nuts or other scrap metal.

Many different baits can be used. Cut fish is a popular one. The bait does not have to reach bottom, since trot lines are generally left out overnight, or longer, and catfish roam and feed freely after dark.

It is possible to buy ready-made trot lines of various lengths, and with varying numbers of dropper lines and hooks.

In open water, away from shore, trot lines are usually set as shown in the illustration—with a buoy of some sort (a large plastic float or a capped plastic jug) at each end. A heavy weight at each end (again, usually a large chunk of scrap metal) holds the line's position.

Sometimes a trot line is tied between two trees or snags, if the particular body of water is suitable. A trot line can also be tied to a tree on the shore; the other end being anchored out in the water.

Be sure to check legal restrictions on trot lines in particular areas. There may be a limit as to length, or the number of hooks, or the type of bait. Trot lines may be prohibited entirely on some bodies of water. Usually, live bait is not allowed.

Fishing Lines

Modern fishing lines are mostly made of synthetic materials—mainly nylon monofilament, braided nylon and braided Dacron. They represent a great improvement over previously-used natural materials, such as cotton, silk and linen. The synthetics don't rot. They need not be dried after each use, and they are generally more uniform in strength and diameter.

BRAIDED NYLON lines are used mostly in certain kinds of casting. Many freshwater plug-casters prefer them, and they are the standard for surf-casting with conventional reels. Braid is softer and "limper" than monofilament, and so spools better on revolving reels. It is less likely to kink or backlash than is monofilament. But, on the other hand, mono is thinner and allows more line to be used on the reel, and is also less visible in the water.

BRAIDED DACRON is used primarily as a saltwater trolling line. For this purpose, it is chosen over braided nylon because it is thinner and has very little stretch.

MONOFILAMENT is the true all-purpose line for modern fishing. It should be used with ALL spinning reels, regardless of size. It is widely used for plug-casting, for ocean trolling, and for saltwater fishing in general. And, of course, monofilament is used for leader material as well as for line.

The choice between Dacron and monofilament for offshore trolling is largely a matter of personal preference. In the 12-, 20-, 30- and 50-pound IGFA line classes, either line can be used, but Dacron is far less "stretchy" than monofilament. It takes an experienced hand to use the light classes of Dacron under conditions of maximum drag pressure and avoid breaking the line. Therefore, it is generally only the expert bluewater angler who chooses Dacron over monofilament in the light and medium classes.

With 80- and 130-pound-class line (possibly even 50), the outlook is different. You're using heavy tackle and strong drag pressure, and the stretchy monofilament line tends to punish the angler too much physically. Besides, the soft Dacron spools and handles far better on the reel when using the thick 80- and 130-pound lines. For these reasons, Dacron is invariably chosen by heavy-tackle anglers who seek marlin and giant tuna.

There is a place, however, for 80- and 100-pound-test monofilament—not for marlin and tuna, but for fishing at great depth in quest of giant snapper, grouper, jewfish and other big but not overly active fish. Mono sinks far faster than Dacron. And you don't worry about the additional burden it imposes on you physically, because that sort of deep fishing requires a strong back no matter how you go about it.

CHOOSING MONOFILAMENT

There are many different brands of monofilament line, and they vary widely in handling qualities. There is really no "best" brand, or type, for all kinds of fishing. And price is not always a reliable guide to the best choice for your own fishing.

As a rule, the highest-priced lines are those which have been highly processed for limpness, and for the smallest ratio of breaking test to line diameter. The limpest lines, of course, are a joy to handle because they lie on the spool beautifully and do not tend to bulge or spring off so much.

For most freshwater fishing, limp lines are much to be preferred.

The saltwater angler, however, soon finds that the ultra-soft monofilaments are not his cup of tea. They "fatigue" or weaken fast under the pressures of big fish, big lures and various other rigors of salty fishing. Also, their knot strength often is below acceptable standards for ocean heavyweights.

Therefore, the saltwater man is quite willing to sacrifice some limpness for lines which better resist abrasion and "fatigue," and which—because they have a slightly harder finish—provide greater knot strength.

Since the major market of nationally-distributed line brands is fresh water, MOST national-brand lines are on the soft side, and therefore less suitable for rugged saltwater fishing than regional brands of line which are distributed mainly in coastal areas.

This is not a hard-and-fast rule as some national brands are entirely satisfactory for coastal work.

HERE'S AN IMPORTANT WORD about line-test: In almost every case, the line you buy will actually test heavier than is stated on the label. This is the way most anglers like it. But if you go in for competitive fishing in clubs and public tournaments, or if you have your eye on possible world records, you want to make sure that your line *does not test heavier* than the allowable limit.

No matter what you may think of the metric system and the anticipated woes of having it jammed down our throats, the first result of metric conversion—to saltwater fishermen, anyway—is a blessing.

The International Game Fish Association, keeper of saltwater records, has adopted the metric system in its line-test classes—not because it's trying to hasten American exposure to these odd tables of weights and measures, but simply because most countries use them already. And the IGFA is, after all, an international body.

Here's how the IGFA now lists its line classes for world records, and the maximum test in each class:

Pounds	Metric (kilograms)	Maximum Test (pounds)
2	1	2.20
4	2	4.40
8	4	8.81
12	6	13.22
16	8	17.63
20	10	22.04
30	15	33.06
50	24	52.91
80	37	81.57
130	60	132.27

Line classes now are labelled by *both* pound-test and kilogram-test. The blessing is that maximum allowable line strength is based on the kilogram class. And this amounts to a liberalization of 10 per cent in maximum test for the lighter line categories.

Before we bog down in decimal points, let's just say that many brands of line you buy nowadays will probably test in their labeled class. Before liberalization, record-size catches made on standard lines often were thrown out because the line overtested. To play it safe, anglers had to pre-test their lines, or else buy special tournament-grade line.

This fiddling with line-test always has been a headache for the record-seeking angler. And even though most saltwater fishermen don't actively seek records, they have frequently run afoul of line-test problems when they happened to catch one.

Avid light-tackle anglers recognized and welcomed the liberalized maximum tests, but failed to take into account the fact that, in all cases, the tests listed are *wet tests*. The IGFA soaks lines before testing—and wet lines lose about 15 per cent of strength. Therefore, anglers who continue to use "tournament" lines are short-changing themselves. They could be using line considerably stronger, yet still safely within allowable limits.

Perhaps the table below will clarify the point.

For comparison, let's look at 12-pound "tournament" line as opposed to the standard 12-pound line in the table below. Usually, 12-pound tournament line will dry-test around 10 pounds. Take away 15 per cent for wet-test, and the actual strength of the line is 8.5—nearly five pounds lighter than is allowed!

Since you pay a premium price for "tournament" line, you'd be dishing out extra money for a severe handicap.

Standard Label	Actual Dry Test Can Be	Wet Test Would Be	Allowable Wet Test Is
2	2.5	2.13	2.2
4	5	4.25	4.4
8	10	8.5	8.8
12	15	12.75	13.22
16	20	17	17.6
20	25	21.3	22
30	38	32.3	33

SPOOLING LINE

No matter what kind of line or what kind of reel you're using, it should be put on the spool under enough pressure to assure that it will not "dig in" to itself. Snug spooling on a spinning reel also helps assure that extra line will not spring off during the cast, and that one or more loops will not spring off simultaneously, thus causing a tangle. On a baitcasting reel or revolving reel of any kind, loosely-spooled line often causes backlashes.

TO INSTALL LINE ON A REVOLVING SPOOL REEL, mount the reel firmly on the rod butt. Have someone hold the spool of line on a pencil or similar object to serve as an axle. Grasp the foregrip of the rod with your left hand, and with the same hand extend your thumb and one or two fingers upward so that you can grasp the line simultaneously. As you crank the reel with your right hand, apply pressure to the line with the fingers of your left hand. You will have to judge the proper amount of pressure; very little is needed for light lines, but with lines of 50-pound or up, you will have to bear down hard and perhaps even wear a glove.

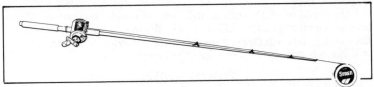

TO INSTALL LINE ON A SPINNING REEL, mount the reel firmly on the rod butt. Grasp the rod *ahead* of the foregrip, and take the line in the same grasp, so that it runs between thumb and one or two fingers. Place your spool of line on the floor. You do not allow the spool to revolve, but merely let the line slip off the end of it. Turn the reel crank as you apply *light* pressure with thumb and finger to the oncoming line. Use just enough pressure to assure a snug wrap. Do not bear down hard, or the monofilament may go on the reel spool in a stretched condition. Later it will try to "un-stretch" itself and return to original shape, thereby exerting great pressure on the spool, and possibly spreading the spool or break-ing it.

Before spooling line in the manner described above, you must check the bail of your reel to see in which direction it travels around your reel spool. Bails on most spinning reels travel in a clockwise direction, therefore the line must slip off the line-spool in a counter-clockwise direction. Otherwise, line twist will result. To change the unwrapping direction from clockwise to counter-clockwise (or vice versa), you have only to turn the spool of line over and let it rest on the opposite end of the spool.

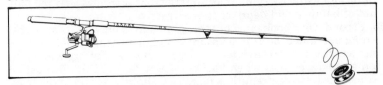

A more satisfactory method of loading line on a spinning reel is to remove the spool from the reel and use a line-winding machine. However, few anglers own such machines. You can, of course, have your spools loaded for you in a tackle store.

Hooks

Choosing a suitable hook for a particular type of fishing is really not such a confusing task as the inexperienced angler might believe. True, the angler is faced with a seemingly endless variation of pattern, finish and size—but he doesn't need a computer in order to make his choices, only a bit of common sense.

First, rid yourself entirely of the notion that an *exact* size of an *exact* pattern is necessary to fishing success. Certain patterns are *desirable* for different specialities, and you have to be somewhere in the neighborhood when it comes to size. But there is a great deal of leeway, as evidenced by the fact that even professional guides may have vastly different ideas as to what makes the best hook for a specific task.

This discussion therefore, will not be overly concerned about trying to sort out subtle differences in the many named patterns on the market, but will stress general characteristics so that the angler will have a guideline for making his own choices.

HOOK SIZES

It helps to understand how hook sizes are designated.

Small hooks are scaled by a system of straight numbers—the larger the number, the smaller the hook. The biggest hook which is labelled by this system is a No. 1. Some very tiny hooks, used mostly for certain demanding types of trout fishing, might wear numbers as high as 20 or 22.

For some strange reason, hooks larger than No. 1 (as almost all saltwater and many freshwater hooks are) wear numbers that begin with No. 1/0, and go *up* as the hook size goes up. The largest size you're ever apt to see in gamefishing is a 20/0.

As already mentioned, you need not trouble yourself over determining an exact size. Usually, the effective range for a specific application spans several sizes. But there are two general considerations that must be taken into account.

First, the size of the hook may well be determined as much by the size of the bait as by the size of the fish you're after. This is particularly true of rigged saltwater baits, but valid in almost any baiting situation. You need a hook which will leave ample point and barb exposure after your bait is fixed to it. On the other hand, you don't want a hook so large that a live bait is unable to swim naturally while carrying it; or so large that it throws a rigged bait out of balance and deprives it of attractive action.

Second, your hook must be strong enough to prevent its straightening out under the drag pressure you plan on using. This factor is not so critical in freshwater and light saltwater fishing with spinning tackle, as it is when you use heavy tackle. Still, it must be considered. Hook strength is increased slightly as size of the hook is increased—but only slightly. In marginal cases you can increase the size of your hook by a couple of numbers and feel safer. But to obtain any drastic change in strength, while keeping the size range within reasonable limits, you'll have to go to a different hook altogether—one of similar size but heavier, sturdier construction.

For anyone using light tackle (all kinds of casting gear, plus ocean tackle with lines up to 30-pound-test) here's a pretty good rule of thumb: When in doubt about choosing from among several available hooks in a range of no more than three size numbers, pick the smallest size.

It is a much more common mistake to use a hook which is too large than one which is too small.

Following are some other hook characteristics which can help you make a common-sense choice.

FRESHWATER HOOKS

Hooks used in freshwater are generally made of lighter wire than hooks designed principally for use in the salt. The usual finish is bronze or blue. Most fishermen feel a subdued tone is less likely to alert a potential biter, especially when using insect baits or bottom baits. Some live-baiters, however, do prefer a nickel-plated or gold-plated hook.

Wading through the numerous patterns of freshwater hooks, we will consider only two basic *designs*. (1) The straight design, where the shank, the bend and the point are in a single plane: that is, if you lay the straight hook flat on a table, the point does not protrude, but lies as flat as the shank. (2) The offset hook, in which the point is bent to one side or other of the shank.

You can compare these two basic designs as follows: Place both hooks flat on a table, then place the palm of your hand over them, and also resting flat. Leave the eyes of both hooks free, outside your hand. Now (gently, of course) try to slide both hooks out from under your hand by pulling on the hook-eyes. The straight hook will slide out. The offset hook will either prick your hand or dig

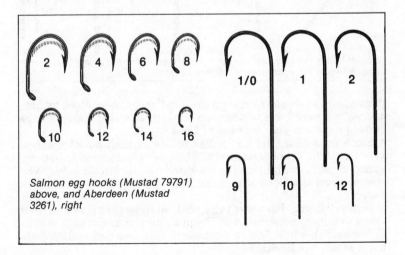

Salmon egg hooks (Mustad 79791) above, and Aberdeen (Mustad 3261), right

51

into the table surface (depending on the direction of the offset). You cannot slide it out.

Thus the offset hook is the choice of many fishermen, because it is less likely to be pulled from a fish's mouth without digging in.

On the other hand, the straight design will *usually* hook a fish, though occasionally it might miss one which an offset would have hooked. The difference in hooking percentage is slight, at best, but enough to swing many folks on the side of the offset.

Offset hooks, however, are not often used on artificial lures because they can affect lure balance and action.

There are numerous style variations, which you can find on hooks of either of the two basic designs—long shanks and short shanks, turned-up eyes and turned-down eyes, straight points and curved points.

Hooks with turned-up or turned-down eyes are used mainly in making certain artificial lures (flies and jigs, mostly). They are of little concern to the bait fisherman.

A long shank hook is more easily removed from a fish after you catch him, and is often an advantage for this reason. But hooks of

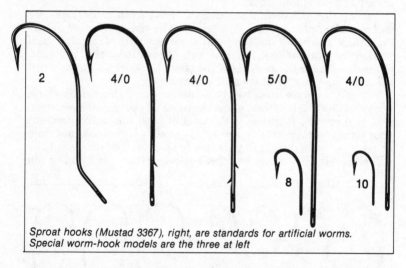

Sproat hooks (Mustad 3367), right, are standards for artificial worms. Special worm-hook models are the three at left

normal and short-shank design are less likely to be noticed by fish, and so you may have to abandon the long-shank if it seems to be cutting down on your number of bites.

Some freshwater fishermen like to use panfish hooks made of very light wire that bends easily. When you get snagged on bottom, extra pressure straightens the hook and allows it to come free. You simply bend the light wire back into proper position and go on fishing.

Naturally, you don't want the hook so light that it might bend when you have a fish on. And if you think you might hook a bass or big catfish while fishing for bream, then you definitely should use a stout-wire hook.

SALTWATER HOOKS

If you haven't already done so, read the discussion of freshwater hooks for a comparison of the straight design and offset design, and for notes on point and eye variations.

Because they are far more likely to corrode, saltwater hooks are generally tinned, nickel-plated, gold-plated, or even made entirely of stainless metal.

In general, offset hooks make excellent choices for still-fishing in salt water with any sort of natural bait, live or dead. Straight-design hooks may be freely substituted for offset hooks in any kind of still-fishing. However, the offset hooks probably have a slightly higher percentage of solid hookups.

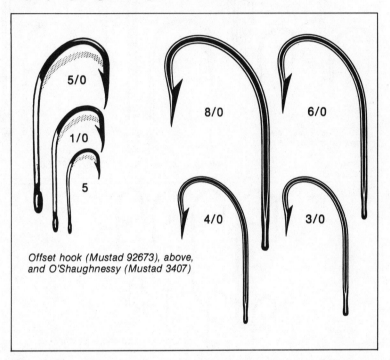

Offset hook (Mustad 92673), above,
and O'Shaughnessy (Mustad 3407)

Straight-design hooks should be used with all *rigged* saltwater baits (strip, ballyhoo, mullet, etc.), because offset hooks sometimes impair trolling action.

Hooks with ringed eyes are used for most inshore fishing, and much offshore fishing as well (with fairly light tackle and reasonably low drag).

Hooks with needle eyes (that is, with the eye drilled through the shank, rather than formed by bending the shank into a circle) are chosen by many offshore fishermen for bluewater trolling and deep bottom fishing, particularly with heavier tackle. The normal ring eye can straighten out under enough strain.

For the really heavy offshore specialties—marlin, shark, tuna, monster bottom fish—you must use a big-game hook, forged of extra-thick metal as added protection against straightening. These can be identified at a glance by their flattened appearance, as well as by size. Naturally, the eyes of big game hooks are also of the

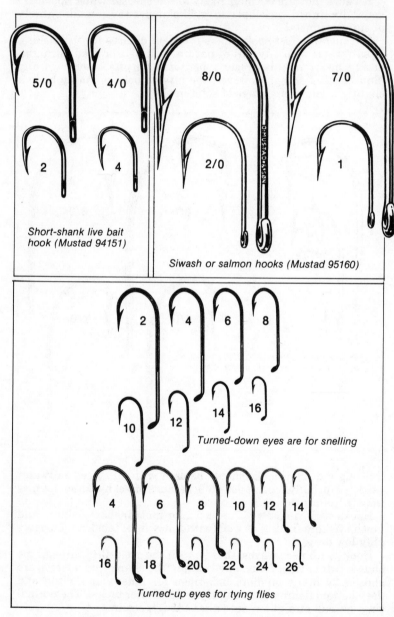

Short-shank live bait hook (Mustad 94151)

Siwash or salmon hooks (Mustad 95160)

Turned-down eyes are for snelling

Turned-up eyes for tying flies

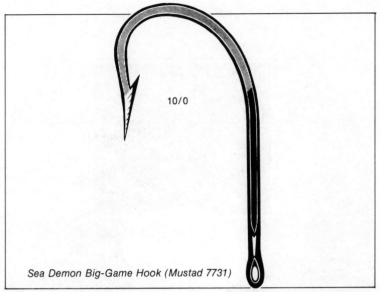

Sea Demon Big-Game Hook (Mustad 7731)

heavy-duty type—either needle-eye, or else a ring-eye that has been braised in closed position for strength. "Monster hooks" of this sort may also be used inshore, for such specialties as big tarpon with heavy tackle, jewfishing, and shark fishing.

Again, there is considerable latitude when it comes to choosing a specific size for certain types of fishing, and much depends on the size of the bait.

WEEDLESS HOOKS

A word must be said about weedless hooks, as these are important to many freshwater fishermen, and are sometimes used in salt water.

The usual weedless hook is nothing more than a familiar style of hook to which has been added an extension of light wire that protects the point, and helps keep it from snagging on weeds or obstructions.

Some artificial lures—usually spoons and spinners, but often flies, jigs and plugs—come equipped with weed guards.

When an angler buys separate weedless hooks, he normally intends to use them for rigging plastic worms. But they can be handy, as well, for fishing minnows and other live baits. Usually, you should hook a minnow or other baitfish through the lips when using a weedless hook.

Sizes of weedless hooks are denoted by the standard system given earlier.

Another type of hook is made weedless by its design, rather than by adding a wire weed guard. In this one, the shank curves abruptly, so that the point is on the same level as the eye. Therefore, the eye and extreme forward portion of the shank serve as a weed guard.

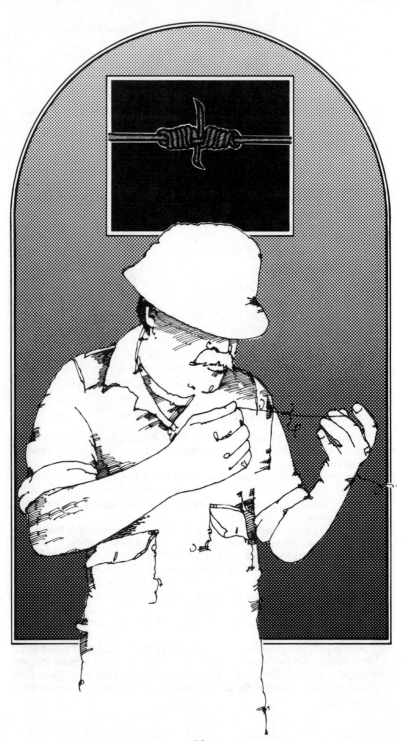

Chapter 2

Baits Rigs & Tackle

Knots & Wire Wraps

Rules of Good Knot Tying

Reliable knots are vital to fish-catching success—and with all kinds of tackle, from the heaviest to the lightest. What makes a good knot? Always consider these three factors:

1. Select a suitable knot for the purpose.
2. Fashion the knot properly.
3. Always draw the knot down snugly, and with even pressure. This is the one step too often overlooked by fishermen. The majority of angling knots (especially if tied with monofilament) are almost

certain to slip and fail unless they are drawn tight to begin with.

All the knots to be given here are tried-and-true ties for the fisherman. They are not the only ones in common use, by any means, but they do represent a complete selection that covers any specialty of sportsfishing rigging you'll encounter.

There are only a few knots which can be tied following a quick glance at the illustration. The proper way to go about learning new knots is to sit down AT HOME with some pieces of line and leader. Look at the illustration, and follow the printed instruction step by step. A modest amount of practice during spare time will assure you of being able to tie the knot you want while out on the water.

Let's go back for a moment to point No. 3 listed earlier, and repeat that all knots should be drawn down snugly. With lighter lines, hand pressure alone can be depended on to tighten the knot sufficiently. When you tie heavy monofilament, however, you often have to grip the hook with pliers to obtain sufficient pressure. And when tying heavy monofilament leader directly to a lighter line, you may have to take a couple of wraps around your hand (use a glove or handkerchief to avoid cuts) before you can draw the knot snug.

Also with heavy monofilaments, the wraps may not lay up close together unless you prod them with a fingernail or blunt instrument as you tighten the knot.

No matter what difficulty you might be having with a particular knot, never try bringing it to final form by jerking sharply. If things aren't going right, start all over. If you jerk while making the knot it will probably break on the spot, and if it doesn't then failure is almost sure to come later at a more unwelcome time.

THE VIC DUNAWAY UNI-KNOT SYSTEM

This unique new system of knot tying enables you to learn just one simple knot formation and adapt it to virtually any knotty need—everything from tying a hook to light line, all the way to joining lines that vary by 10 times in test.

Not only is this system the first unified approach to knot tying, but it also provides 100 per cent knot strength in most of its applications. The few finished ties which do not test a full 100 per cent still test consistently at 90 per cent or higher. Moreover, the strength of the Uni-Knot isn't diminished when the line is broken with a jerk, rather than with steady pressure. Some knots which test 100 per cent on a steady pull will break at 50 or 60 per cent if subjected to severe and sudden jolts—such as might be administered by a big fish striking close to boatside, or by the angler himself, if he gets too muscular in trying to set a hook. The Spider Hitch and Palomar are examples of apparently top-strength knots which break all too easily on a severe shock.

The practiced knot-tying expert will simply add the Uni-Knot system to his personal inventory of ties, using elements of it for particular applications, and other knots, at times, for other applications.

But for most fishermen, who are looking for the easiest way to handle their knot needs, the Uni-Knot System is the only thing they really need to learn.

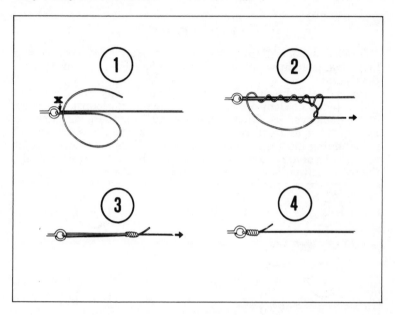

LEARNING THE SYSTEM

The one knot requirement basic to all fishermen is that of tying a line to the eye of a hook or swivel. Familiarize yourself with the simple procedure of using the Uni-Knot for this purpose, and then all other Uni-Knot applications become quite easy.

First, run the line through the eye for several inches. Turn the end back toward the eye to form a circle as shown in picture No. 1. With thumb and finger of the left hand, grasp both strands of line and the crossing strand in a single grip at the point marked X— just forward of the hook. Now, make six turns with the end around both strands of line and through the circle, as in picture No. 2.

Maintaining the same grip with the left hand, pull on the end of the line in the direction shown by the arrow until all the wraps are snugged tight and close together. Snugging down tightly at this stage is essential to maximum knot strength. If you make six turns and snug the knot very tightly, you'll consistently get 100 per cent of line strength.

Finally, slide the finished knot tight against the eye of the hook by dropping the end and then pulling on the standing part of the line as shown by the arrow in picture No. 3. The excess end can be trimmed flush with the knot after final positioning (picture No. 4).

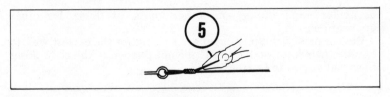

END LOOP

It takes just one slight variation to transform the hook tie into a loop arrangement which provides more freedom of action for artificial lures.

Instead of sliding the finished knot all the way to the eye, just slide it to the size loop desired. Then, gripping the loop just forward of the hook eye, take hold of the tag end with pliers, as shown in picture No. 5, and pull very hard. This locks the Uni-Knot around the standing line (or leader) at that point. If it slides down at all it will only be under heavy pressure when fighting a fish. Meanwhile, the loop position is maintained while casting and retrieving.

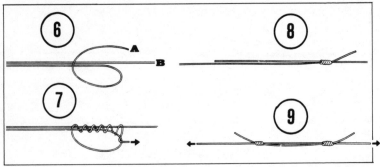

LINE TO LINE

Tying line to line is actually done the same way as tying line to hook. Compare picture No. 1 with picture No. 6 and you can see that you handle things the same way, even though the two parallel strands involved are from different pieces of line, rather than from the same piece doubled back.

The procedure is simply to form the Uni-Knot circle with line A around line B, going through six times and pulling down as in picture No. 7. Once the knot is formed and tightened (No. 8), you then have to reverse the lines and tie another Uni-Knot with line B around line A. After the two knots are finished, pull on the two main strands of line, as indicated by arrows in picture No. 9, to slide the two knots together. Trim both excess ends.

This application replaces the Blood Knot, which is one of the most difficult of all knots to handle. Breaking strength of this tie is less than 100 per cent, but over 90 per cent and consistently stronger than the Blood Knot. It can be increased to 100 per cent if you double both strands of line before tying the pair of Uni-Knots, but the single tie is strong enough for all practical purposes.

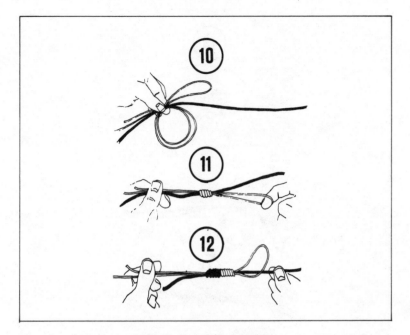

LINE TO LEADER

Tying light line to heavy leader is not much different from the preceding application. It may *seem* awkward at first because the end of the light line must be doubled to gain maximum strength. But the doubled portion is treated as a single strand and is actually easier to draw down.

Double back several inches of line. Overlap the doubled section with the end of the heavy leader and form the familiar Uni-Knot circle, as in picture No. 10. Go around the strands and through the the circle with the doubled end. It is only necessary to go through three times. Now, slip your finger into the loop. Holding all strands on the other side of the knot with the left hand, pull the loop with your finger until the knot is very snug (picture No. 11).

Reverse the lines and tie another Uni-Knot with the end of the heavy leader around *both* strands of line (there are two strands because the light line is doubled). Again, only three turns are required. Pull the second knot down as snugly as you can manage.

Last, slide the knots together by pulling with opposing pressure on the main strand of leader and *both* strands of line (picture No. 12). Continue pulling hard until no slippage is felt. For final tightening, you will probably have to grip the line with a full hand grip, instead of using thumb-finger grips.

This tie will consistently provide 100 per cent of line strength *if* the first Uni-Knot is snugged completely tight, and *if* final tightening is done carefully and with steady hard pressure.

As with all other monofilament knots, improper tying reduces strength.

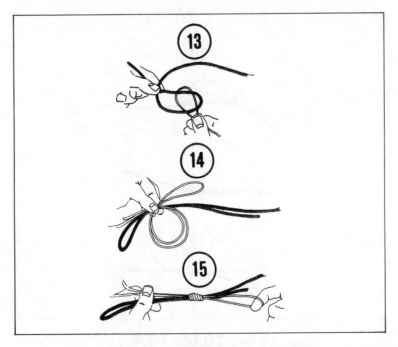

LINE TO LEADER ALTERNATE

This is a different line-to-leader tie that should be used when diameters of the two monofilaments involved vary by five times or more in test. It makes a much trimmer tie than the previous one when you use extremely thick leader. And note that it should be used *only* with greatly differing diameters, since the bulk of the larger leader is needed to provide a positive hold.

Double both the light line and heavy leader. Insert the doubled line through the leader loop *upward,* as in picture No. 13. Make the Uni-Knot circle, grip all strands with thumb and finger (No. 14) and then make four turns through the circle. Holding all strands with the left hand, insert finger in loop of light line and draw the Unit-Knot down very tight (No. 15) around both strands of heavy leader.

Last step is to take a firm grip on *both* strands of light line but only the *main* strand of leader and pull until the knot slides to the doubled end of the leader. Continue pulling hard until no more slippage is felt, then trim off all excess ends.

Key to successful tying of this one is pulling the knot down completely tight before sliding it to the end. If you feel it's sliding too easily, the knot probably isn't tight enough, and it should be retightened before pulling it to final position.

Done properly, this also is a consistent 100 per cent tie, and can be used with seemingly incredible variations in size—for instance, one-pound-test line to 100-pound-test leader.

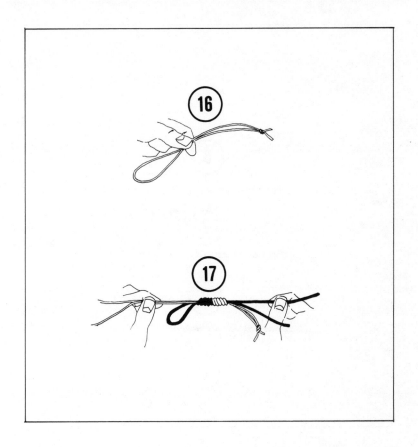

REPLACING THE BIMINI TWIST

To form a maximum strength double-line, you must use a simple but back-door approach. First you cut off enough line to form the desired length of double line, and tie the ends together with an overhand knot as shown in picture No. 16. Then you proceed to tie the double-line back onto your line. The overhand knot is for convenience only and will be trimmed away later.

Double the end of the standing line. The procedure that follows is just the same as the line-to-line tie illustrated with pictures No. 6 through 9. The obvious and only difference is that you're working with two double strands instead of two single strands.

There is one idiosyncrasy, however, that must be catered to in order to get a 100 per cent result. After the two knots are pulled together until they just touch, the final tightening must be done by pulling with both strands of double-line, but only the main strand of regular line, as in picture No. 17.

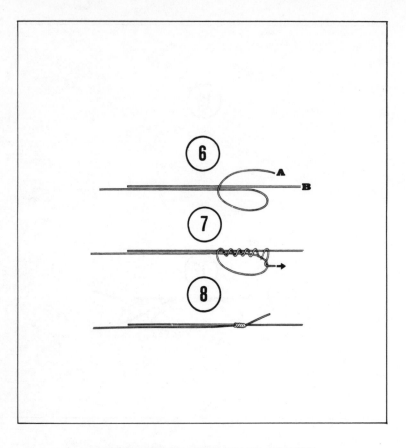

REPLACING THE NAIL KNOT

You can tie a leader to your fly line in seconds with the Uni-Knot, achieving the identical result as with the tedious Nail Knot that requires a tapered nail or tube for tying.

Again, refer to pictures 6 through 8, but assume that line B is your fly line and line A is your leader.

The formation doesn't change at all. However, when you pull the leader knot down around the fly line, you'll have to do it in three or four stages, prodding the wraps together with your thumb in between the stages. This is because the fly line's soft coating does not allow the wraps to be pulled together in a single sweep.

Once you have pulled and prodded the wraps together, getting a result similar to that shown in picture No. 8, grasp the tag end of the leader with pliers. Holding the main strand of leader with your left hand, pull hard with the pliers to make the knot "bite" into the fly line's coating. This is what holds the knot in place. A second Uni-Knot isn't necessary. Trim off the excess ends of leader and fly line as close to the knot as possible, and you have the neatest of all fly leader ties, done in a few seconds.

SNELLING A HOOK

Snelling is a snap with the Uni-Knot. Thread line through the hook eye, pulling through at least six inches. Form the familiar Uni circle and hold it tight against the hook shank with thumb and finger. Make several turns (four or five are enough) around the shank and through the circle. Pull on tag end to draw knot roughly closed. Finish by holding the standing line in one hand, the hook in the other, and pulling in opposite directions.

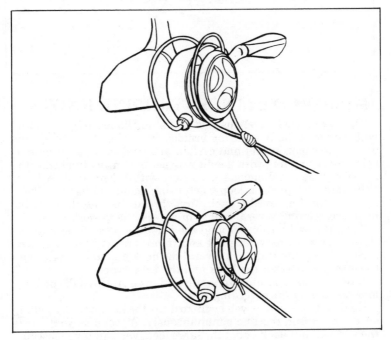

SPOOLING LINE

To affix line to a revolving spool reel for filling, pass the end of the line around the spool. Grasp the tag end and the standing line with thumb and finger of left hand, and tie a Uni-Knot. Trim the knot close, then pull gently on the standing line to snug the loop tight to the spool.

For a spinning reel spool, simply make a large loop in the end of the line with a Uni-Knot, drop the loop over the spool, and draw it up by pulling on the standing line. In either case, use only two or three wraps to form the Uni.

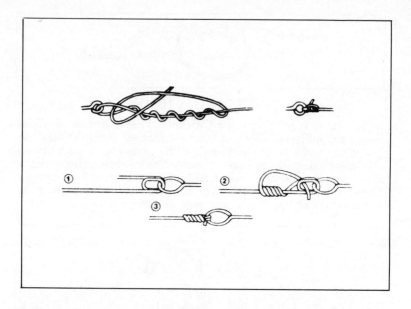

IMPROVED CLINCH, TRILENE KNOTS

This is the most widely used of all fishing knots, and works well with either monofilament or braided line. Use it for tying line directly to hook, swivel and certain artificial lures, such as jigs, spinners or any lure with a split-ring permanently attached to the lure-eye. Plugs and spoons work best with a loop knot. A lot of fishermen also prefer a loop when using lead-head jigs.

To tie the Improved Clinch, first thread the line through the hook eye, leaving several inches of excess line to work with.

Wrap the end portion around the standing part of the line five times. Fewer wraps weaken the knot; more wraps are unnecessary.

Next, bring the end back toward the hook and insert it through the opening between the hook and the first wrap.

Now turn the end upward again and insert it through the large loop created by the preceding step.

Hold on to the end as you begin to draw the knot tight by pulling on the hook and the line simultaneously. As soon as you're sure the end will not back out of the large loop, you can turn loose and finish the job of drawing tight.

The loose end should be trimmed to about an eighth-inch in length. It should not be trimmed flush with the knot.

The Trilene knot, researched and recommended by the manufacturers of Trilene monofilament lines, is a variation on the Improved Clinch in which the tag end is run through the eye twice (1) and then passed through the resulting double opening just forward of the eye (2). This gives strength and dependability without having to turn and go through the large loop, as in the Improved Clinch. Simply draw the knot tight (3) after completing step 2.

66

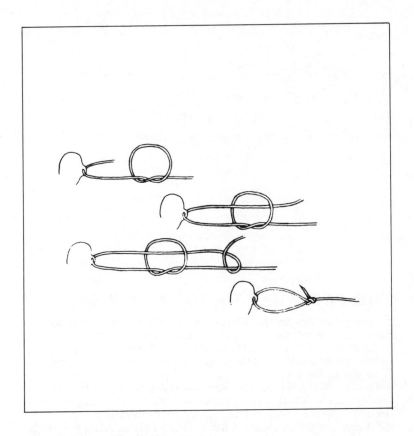

THE END-LOOP KNOT

This knot can be used for tying a lure to the end of monofilament leader material that is heavier than your line. It is a fast knot to tie, and it affords the necessary freedom of lure action which is so vital to the productivity of many plugs. Do not use this knot for tying a lure directly to light line, because it weakens the line-test too much. Instead, use the TWO-WRAP HANGMAN'S KNOT, which will be described next, or the UNI-KNOT LOOP.

First, and before you put the line through the eye of the lure, tie a simple overhand knot several inches from the end, but do not close the overhand knot at this point.

Second, go through the lure eye, turn, and insert the end of the line through the wide portion of the overhand knot.

The exact size of the final loop is determined at this stage by drawing the overhand knot as close to the lure as you want it.

Finally, make a simple half-hitch with the end of the line around the standing part of the line ABOVE the overhand knot. Pull tight with pressure on the lure and on the line.

Trim, leaving about an eighth-inch end.

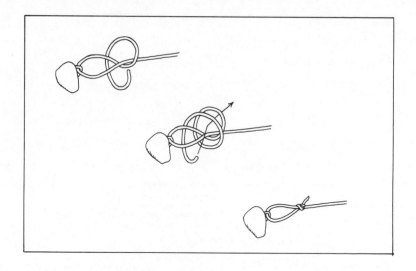

THE TWO-WRAP HANGMAN'S KNOT

Fishing guides in the Florida Keys refer to this knot as the figure eight knot; however, it is different from another and more commonly-used knot which is also called the figure-eight, but which can be used only with certain types of wire. (See chapter on Wire Wraps for that one.)

The Two-Wrap Hangman's Knot results in a slipping loop, which can be tightened at any point to provide the size loop-opening desired. The loop will remain open while casting, but will close tight against the eye when a fish is being fought. After the catch, it can easily be opened again (better re-tied if the leader has been frayed even slightly).

This knot can be used with either heavy or light monofilament, and is preferable to the End-Loop Knot (described previously) when no heavy leader is being used, because it retains a much higher percentage of breaking test.

First, thread the line through the eye, allowing youself several inches to work with.

Now make two wraps back toward the lure-eye (not away from the eye as with the Improved Clinch). Keep these two wraps as loose as possible—holding them open with thumb and finger.

Next, thread the end of the line back through the two wraps, away from the lure-eye and parallel to the standing line.

To tighten this knot it is now necessary to stick the lure into something rigid (such as a boat cleat, tree branch, etc.). After the hook is so fixed, grip the excess end of line with a pair of pliers.

Now pull simultaneously on the line with your hand, and on the excess end with the pliers. You'll note that the knot now slips up and down. Position the loop as you want it, then tighten firmly with extra pressure from the pliers.

Trim, leaving an eighth-inch end.

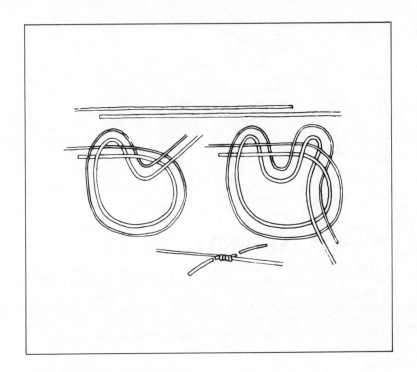

SURGEON'S KNOT

This is a fast, easy and reliable knot for tying a heavy monofilament leader, or shock line, directly to either monofilament or braided fishing line. It can be used for line and leader of greatly differing diameter, although the practical limit is roughly five times line test—that is, 4-lb. line to 20-lb. leader; 8-lb. to 40-lb.; 10-lb. to 50-lb., etc.

If your diameters differ more than that, it will probably be better to use the Albright Special.

Even though this is one of the easiest of all knots to tie, it is difficult to illustrate plainly. So don't be alarmed. Follow both the illustration and instruction, and you'll be tying it in a few seconds.

First, lay out the leader parallel to the line, letting the end of the line and the end of the leader overlap for six or eight inches.

Now, treating both strands as one, tie a simple overhand knot in the doubled section, making sure that both the short end (line) and long end (leader) are pulled completely through. Do not tighten the knot at this point.

Next, simply go through again with both ends, exactly as before, again making certain both ends are pulled through.

Finally draw the knot tight by gripping BOTH STRANDS on either side of the knot, and drawing down with steady pressure.

The ends of this knot may be trimmed flush with the wraps.

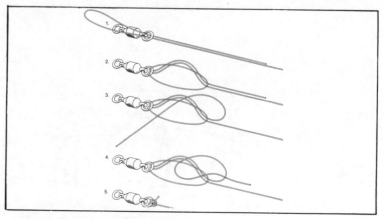

WORLD'S FAIR KNOT

This knot resulted from DuPont Stren's first "Great Knot Search" contest and was announced at the Knoxville World's Fair in 1982. The winner was Gary L. Martin of Lafayette, La. To tie, pass the doubled end through the eye (1) and fold it back (2). Next, run the tag end under the doubled strands and over the loop (3). Finally, run the tag end through the loop formed by step 3 (4) and draw tight (5).

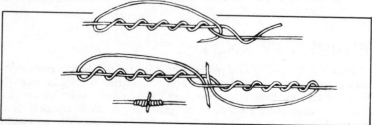

BLOOD KNOT

Best uses for the Blood Knot are to re-tie a broken spinning line; to add more line to your reel spool; or to join tapered sections of fly-fishing leaders. In other words, the Blood Knot is useful mainly for joining together monofilaments of the same, or only slightly differing, diameters.

First, overlap both sections of line, end to end, and then wrap one section around the other five times.

Next, wrap the remaining end around the other section—also five times but in the opposite direction.

Now insert both ends back through the center opening, again in opposite directions.

The knot is pulled tight by drawing on the lines at either side of the knot. Care must be taken at this point to prevent the ends from backing out of the center insert.

Trim, leaving an eighth-inch end.

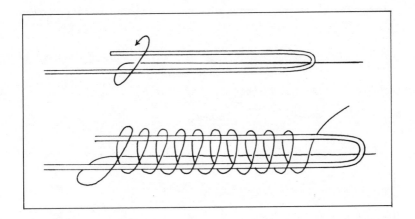

ALBRIGHT SPECIAL

When you wish to tie a light monofilament line directly to a very heavy monofilament leader (for instance, 10-lb. to 80-lb.) this is the knot to master. It has the added advantage of being a slim and neat tie that will generally slip through the rod guides if you wish to crank the knot past the rod tip.

The Albright Special also is used for tying light line directly to wire cable, nylon-coated wire or even to single-strand wire leader in the smaller diameters.

This knot is tricky at first, and may take some practice. However, it really isn't very difficult once you get the hang of it.

First, double back a couple inches of the heavy material.

Insert the line through the loop which is thus formed. Pull 10 or 12 inches of line through to give yourself ample line to work with.

Now you must wrap the line back over itself, and over both strands of the doubled leader. While doing this, you are gripping the line and both leader strands together with the thumb and finger of your left hand, and winding with your right. Make 15 turns, then insert the end of the line back through the loop once more at the point of the original entry.

Before turning loose your thumb-and-finger grip, pull gently on the standing part of the line to remove slack; then pull gently on the short end of the leader to close the loop; then pull gently on the short end of the line to remove more slack.

Finally comes the last stage of tightening. Pull the short end of the line as tight as you possibly can. Then pull the standing part of the line tight.

Clip off the excess line, leaving about an eighth-inch end. Clip off the excess from the leader loop, again leaving a very slight protrusion.

SPECIAL NOTE: The Albright Special, in particular, is a knot which must be tied with great care. Practice it thoroughly at home. But, as mentioned before, once you learn it, it seems surprisingly quick and simple.

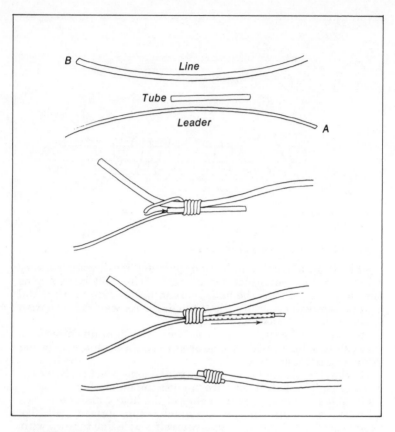

TUBE OR NAIL KNOT

This one is used to tie a leader butt directly to your fly line. Originally, a nail was used to tie this knot—with the leader being inserted in the small space between nail and line.

By using a small tube instead of a nail, it is much easier to insert the leader back underneath all the wraps. Any small-diameter tube can be used—a hypodermic needle, the refill barrel of a ball-point pen (cleaned out, of course), etc.

First, lay out the fly line and leader as in illustration. Grip all three with thumb and finger of left hand.

Take the leader at point A with your right hand, and wrap back toward the end of the fly line (B), making five snug wraps.

Now, run the end of the leader (A again) back through the tube.

Slide the tube out in the direction of the arrow, and tighten the knot by pulling on both ends of the leader. Pull the leader down very tight—using pliers to grip the short end if necessary.

Do not pull on the fly line until after the leader is pulled down tight and bites into the coating of the fly line!

Once the knot is tight, the excess end of the fly line, and of the leader, can be trimmed short.

72

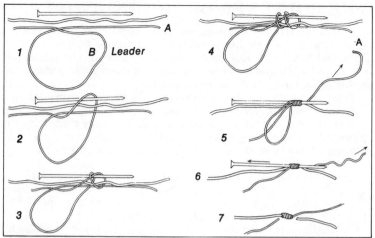

1 B Leader A

2

3

4 A

5

6

7

FAST NAIL KNOT

These instructions outline a new and drastically-improved method for tying the Nail Knot. The knot itself is used to tie a permanent leader butt onto the end of a fly line (for instructions on making fly-fishing leaders see Chapter 3).

The old method of tying this knot required the use of a specially-tapered nail, or a small hollow tube—and the tying consumed several minutes, even if the angler was completely familiar with the procedure.

With this new method, you can use any small-diameter object—a nail, needle, or even a matchstick or toothpick. It serves only as a "stiffener" to make wrapping easier.

First, make a circle with the leader, as shown in the illustration.

Using the thumb and forefinger of your left hand, take all the components in a single grip—nail, fly line, and both overlapping ends of the leader.

Now you do not wrap with any of the ends. You wrap instead with the right-side arc of the leader circle. Grasp this about in the middle (B) with your right hand, and make five snug turns simultaneously around the nail, the fly line and the leader, working back toward your left hand.

When the five turns have been made, let your left thumb-and-finger grip slide over the wraps to hold them tight.

Now use your right hand to grasp the leader end (A) and pull it all the way through until the circle is closed and the knot comes tight.

Remove the nail, and finish tightening the knot by pulling on both ends of the leader. Take care that when you remove the nail, the fly line doesn't slide out of the wraps as well.

As a last step, tighten the knot some more. Use pliers to get a good grip on the short end of the leader. The knot must be pulled tight enough so that it presses firmly into the coating of the fly line.

With clippers, trim the short end of the leader and the short end of the line as close as you can to the knot.

THE ROLLOVER OR "BIMINI TWIST"

The Rollover Knot has long been employed by big-game fishermen to form a double line—either 15 feet long with lines through 50-pound-test, or 30 feet long with lines exceeding 50-pound-test (those being the maximum double-line lengths allowed under International Game Fish Association rules).

The value of the double line in big-game fishing is this: When a fish has been brought to boatside, the double line is by then wrapped for a few turns onto the reel. This means that twice the pressure can be applied to keep the fish from bolting, and also that the angler has twice the margin of protection against line breakage at the critical gaffing stage.

In recent years, the Rollover Knot has been widely adopted by spin, plug and fly fishermen—not to provide long length of double line, but to assure *maximum possible knot strength*. A properly-tied Rollover Knot always is stronger than the line.

Normally, the light-tackle folks use the Rollover to make no more than two or three feet of double line. This doubled line then is tied directly to the leader (using the Albright Special or Surgeon's Knot) or else a swivel (using the Improved Clinch Knot).

Any fisherman's knot can be tied with a double line as easily as with a single line.

For most freshwater and inshore fishing, where line-test is reasonably well matched to the fish generally encountered, it is not necessary to rig with the double line. Knots such as the Surgeon's and Improved Clinch afford about 85 per cent of line test when used with the single line, and this is ample for run-of-the-mill fishing.

On the other hand, double line should always be used with any kind of tackle and in any kind of fishing where your line is likely to be put to the full test of its strength. Following are a few examples: all offshore fishing; tarpon fishing with fly, plug or spin tackle, or with light general tackle; snook fishing in tight quarters, such as mangrove creeks or around pilings; all kinds of saltwater fly casting where a heavy tippet is employed; deep-jigging and other deep-sea, light-tackle specialties.

TYING THE ROLLOVER

This is one knot which really is difficult for the fellow who hasn't tied it before. But, once learned, it can be tied in less than a minute —and take heart at the knowledge that hundreds of fishermen now tie it regularly, even in a rocking boat. You can too, if you practice and master it at home.

The one most important thing to remember when tying the rollover is to keep pressure at all times on all three points—1. The standing line above the knot. 2. The end of line which you're working with. 3. The terminal end of the loop.

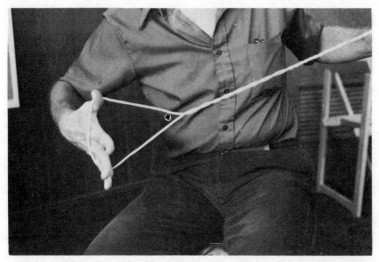

Photo No. 1—Double the end of your line, making the doubled portion about three feet long. Insert your hand in the loop and make 20 complete revolutions with your hand to form the 20 wraps. Note that at this stage, the wraps are spread over a considerable portion of the line.

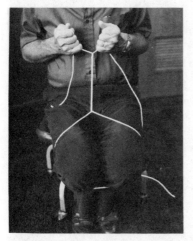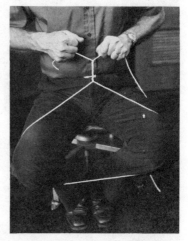

Photo No. 2—Sitting erect, hold your knees tightly together and place the loop over them. Maintain pressure, as shown, with your hands on both the standing line and the short end.

Photo No. 3—Spread your knees slowly, maintaining very tight hand pressure in opposing directions, as before. This will draw the wraps tightly together.

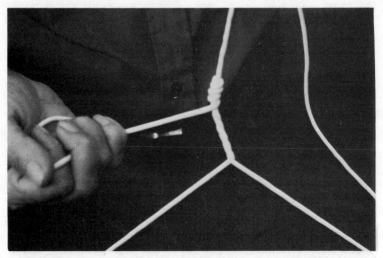

Photo No. 4—Once the wraps are very snug, pull slightly downward with the short end while relaxing tension slightly at the same time. Be sure to keep up the tension, however, with the left hand and with the knees. The line should then roll easily over the wraps, all the way down to the end.

Photo No. 5—This shows the completed rollover before it is anchored with a half-hitch around one strand, and several half-hitches around both strands. IMPORTANT NOTE: This photo is somewhat deceiving, in that it shows the rollover wraps lying perfectly parallel and snug against each other. Your finished wrap may show a considerably more spiralled look. This is perfectly O.K., so long as all wraps are tight.

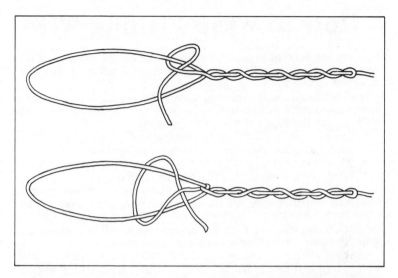

Step No. 6 (Drawing)—This shows detail of finishing half hitches: the first around a single strand, and three others around both strands. Trim, leaving about an eighth-inch end.

ADDITIONAL NOTES ON THE ROLLOVER—Obviously, the steps illustrated here are for making a short double line for use with casting tackle. To make 15 or 30 feet of double line for big-game fishing, two people should be involved. One man handles the mechanics of forming the knot, while the other spreads the two strands of double line and maintains tension on them. In short, the second man (with his hands) performs the same function that your knees did while making the short double line.

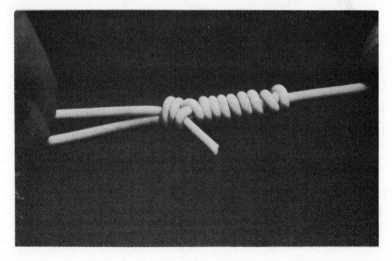

How to Wrap Fishing Wire

There are several types of fishing wire, and the purpose of this section is merely to give instruction as to how each type should be wrapped onto a hook, lure or swivel.

Instructions on how to choose among the various types and sizes of wire, and their uses as fishing leaders, are covered in Chapter 3.

These are the types of wire in regular use:

1. Stainless steel single-strand leader wire.
2. Monel single-strand trolling wire (wire line).
3. Wire cable, formed of twisted wire filaments, for leaders.
4. Wire cable, coated with plastic, for leaders.

Every type comes in a great range of diameters. When working with single-strand wire, all diameters are wrapped in exactly the same way; however, the larger the wire, the more difficult it will be to wrap. When working with the larger sizes, it will be necessary to grip your loop with pliers as you make the wrap.

Cutting pliers, obviously, are a necessity when working with wire. They will be needed to cut the desired length of wire from your coil or spool. In some cases (mostly with cable) cutters are used to trim the end after the wrap. But single-strand wire should be BROKEN, not cut, or a tiny sharp end will be left, which can rip a careless hand.

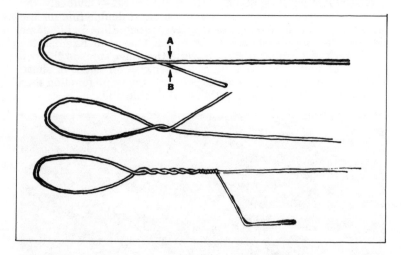

THE HAYWIRE TWIST

For top strength and reliability, the Haywire Twist should be the standard wrap with single-strand leader wire or Monel wire line in virtually all types of saltwater fishing. Experience has DEFINITELY PROVED that simple overhand wire wraps will invariably pull out under heavy pressure. For light inshore fishing with spinning tackle, the overhand wrap will usually hold up—but even there you run the risk of losing an exceptional fish due to prolonged strain.

Though instructions are given for the overhand wrap, it is strongly recommended that everyone learn the Haywire Twist and use it as common practice for any kind of wire-leader fishing.

Here's how it's done:

Start by forming the desired size loop. You may simply make a loop for later attachment to a snap, or you may run the wire through the eye of hook or swivel. In either case, the procedure is the same.

Cross the strands as shown. Hold loop tightly with fingers of left hand, or with pliers. Using right hand, press DOWN at point A with forefinger, and at the same time press UP at point B with thumb.

The second illustration shows how the wire should look after the first twist. Using exactly the same procedure, repeat three or four times.

After making the series of Haywire Twists, finish off by wrapping the short end around the standing leader as snugly as possible. This finishing wrap does not add strength, but is necessary to keep the Haywire from unwrapping.

BREAK THE WIRE by bending a "crank handle" in the surplus end, as shown. Then, while holding the loop tightly in the left hand, crank this handle in a full circular motion. The surplus will snap off neatly at the last wrap.

If you have difficulty breaking the wire in this manner it is probably because you are making the circular motion in the same direction as you made the wrap. You must let your circular sweep run PARALLEL to the standing part of the wire—not AROUND the standing wire.

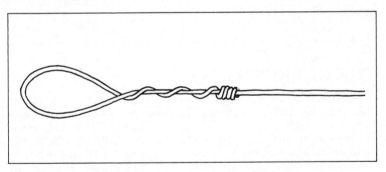

OVERHAND WIRE WRAP

The Overhand Wrap is nothing more than the final stage of the Haywire Twist. You merely run the end of the wire through the hook eye, then bend it back and wrap the short end around the long end several times.

Finish off by breaking the wire as directed previously.

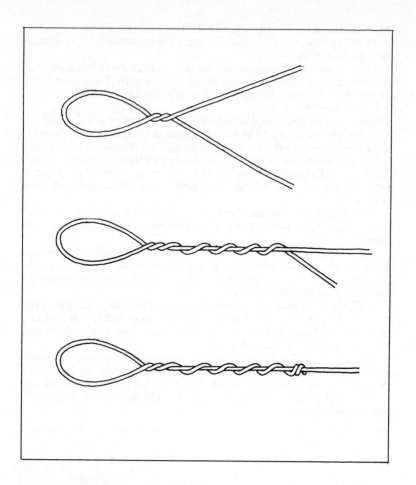

THE GREENE TWIST

Developed by expert angler Tom Greene of Lighthouse Point, Fla., this wire twist, amazing as it seems, gives an extra measure of breaking safety over the traditional Haywire Twist. This extra margin means little in routine angling, especially with light and medium tackle, and when fish are netted or gaffed. However, in big-game fishing, when the leader must be handled by a mate to bring the fish within range of a flying gaff or the tagging stick, then the Greene Twist is a surer bet to withstand the extra pressure.

First form the loop or run the wire through the hook eye, as the case may be, and then begin the wrap exactly the same as for the Haywire; however, you make only two Haywire wraps. Next, wrap the tag end around the standing wire five or six times very loosely —so loosely that it would unwind if you let it go. Last, complete with two—and two only—overhand wraps as with the Haywire, and break off the tag end.

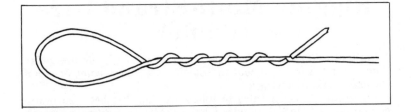

THE QUICK-CHANGE WIRE WRAP

Here is a useful wrap for the fellow who casts with light spinning or baitcasting tackle and likes the convenience of fast lure change.

You start out as if making the regular overhand wrap, but you spiral the wraps widely four or five times.

The surplus must be cut with pliers: however, if you're careful to cut right on the last bend, the danger of a sharp end is lessened.

To change lures, unwrap the wide spirals, put on the new lure, and wrap the whole thing closed again. It takes but a few seconds.

Though not as reliable as a Haywire, the wide spiral twist is surprisingly strong—much stronger than the tight overhand.

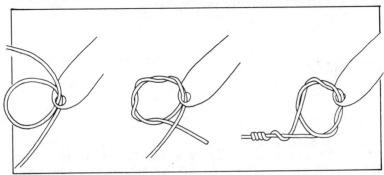

SPECIAL SPOON WRAP

Here's a nifty system for attaching a trolling spoon to your wire leader. It gives the spoon much more action in the water, and is widely used by commercial kingfishermen and by guides.

Run your leader wire through the eye of the spoon, pulling several inches of wire through. Turn the end of the wire and go through the eye again, same way as before.

Now you see that a circle of wire has been formed. Run the end of your wire through this circle several times, until you go completely around the circle and get back to the standing part of the leader wire. Now make your Haywire Twist, finish the regular wrap and break off the surplus wire as usual.

NOTE: Immediately after forming the circle, and before beginning any wraps, adjust the size of the circle to desired diameter by pulling on the loose end of wire. The diameter usually is about a half-inch.

Rigging Multi-Strand Wire (Cable)

Multi-strand twisted wire is commonly used for leader material. Some of it has a nylon coating (Steelon, Sevalon); some does not (Sevenstrand, Steelstrand).

There are no strict rules to follow in choosing between multi-strand and single-strand wire for your metallic leaders, although general guidelines are offered at the beginning of the chapter on "Leaders."

All but one of the connections to be described here may be used with either plain or nylon-coated cable. The one exception is the match method, usable only with nylon coating.

SLEEVE AND CRIMPER

This is probably the most widely used method of attaching cable wire to a hook or swivel. Both the sleeves and crimping tool (crimping pliers) may be purchased at most tackle stores. The sleeves come in a variety of sizes, so be sure to select the proper size for the leader material you plan to use. Any dealer who sells sleeves should have a chart describing the proper sizes.

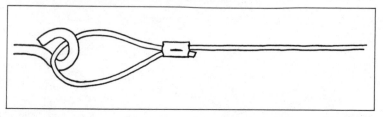

SINGLE SLEEVE RIG—One sleeve may be used with light cable wire for light-duty fishing. To rig, simply thread the sleeve onto the wire, then run the end of the wire through the eye of your hook, and then back through the sleeve. Adjust to the desired size loop, crimp the sleeve, and trim off excess wire.

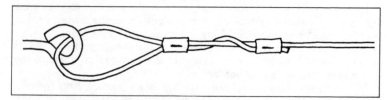

DOUBLE SLEEVE RIG—For added protection against failure (and especially with larger sizes of cable), use two sleeves. Start by crimping on the first sleeve as described in the preceding paragraph. Then wrap the excess end once or twice around the standing part of the leader and thread it through a second sleeve. Last, crimp the second sleeve and trim off excess wire.

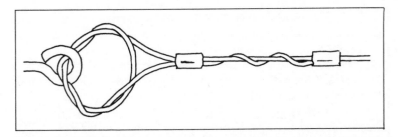

CIRCLE WRAP WITH DOUBLE SLEEVE FOR HEAVY BIG GAME FISHING—This connection is the choice of many big-game fishermen who seek the largest marlin with 80- or 130-pound-test line. It provides maximum protection against weakening and breaking during a high-pressure fight that could easily last several hours. These anglers prefer heavy cable over heavy single-strand wire because it is not so apt to kink and snap. The connection is made by running the wire TWICE through the eye of hook or swivel. This forms a circle of wire. Run the end of the wire through the circle (the circle should be small—½-inch or less in diameter) three or four times, or until the end of the wire gets back to the standing part. Now wrap the end once around the leader, slip the first sleeve over this wrap, and crimp it. Last, wrap the end three or four times around the leader and crimp on the second sleeve. (NOTE: For detail drawing on how to form the wire circle, see the illustration entitled SPOON WRAP in the section on rigging single-strand wire.)

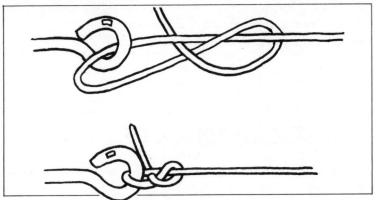

FIGURE-EIGHT KNOT

Light cable or nylon-covered cable may be tied directly to lure, hook or swivel by using this simple yet strong knot. You merely wrap the end once around the leader, then thread it back through the first opening—as shown in the illustration. Use pliers to hold the end as you pull the knot tight.

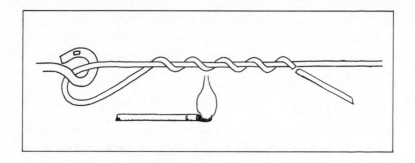

THE MATCH METHOD

A simple system for securing nylon-coated cable to a hook or swivel is shown in the illustration. Run the end through the eye, then wrap it three or four times around the leader. Leave a couple of inches excess so you can hold the wraps in place without getting your fingers close to the fire. Now strike a match and pass the flame quickly back and forth along the wraps until the nylon melts and fuses. Do not hold the flame against the wraps too long or the nylon will melt away completely! After fusion is complete, trim off the excess end of wire.

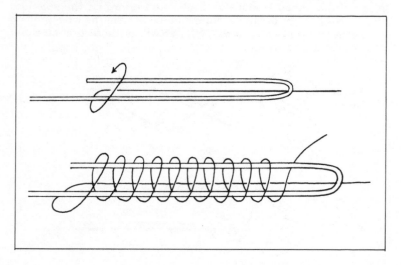

TYING CABLE TO MONOFILAMENT

Cable or nylon-coated cable in the smaller diameters can be tied directly to monofilament line or leader by using the Albright Special Knot. Simply double the wire end about one inch, then tie the Albright as described in an earlier section.

WIRE LEADER SIZES (CABLE)

Table is for Sevenstrand

Size (pound test)	Diameter
18	.011
27	.012
40	.015
60	.018
90	.024
135	.029
170	.033
250	.039

WIRE LEADER SIZES (NYLON-COATED CABLE)

Table is for Sevalon

Size (pound test)	Diameter
18	.018
27	.020
40	.024
60	.034
90	.048
135	.058
170	.065
250	.075

WIRE LEADER SIZES (SINGLE-STRAND)

No.	Diameter	Lb. Test
2	.011	28
3	.012	32
4	.013	39
5	.014	54
6	.016	61
7	.018	72
8	.020	88
9	.022	108
10	.024	127
12	.029	184
15	.035	258
19	.043	352

WIRE LEADER SIZES (AIRCRAFT CABLE)

Table is for Duratest

Size (pound test)	Diameter
175	.036
275	.042
400	.053
600	.067
800	.092

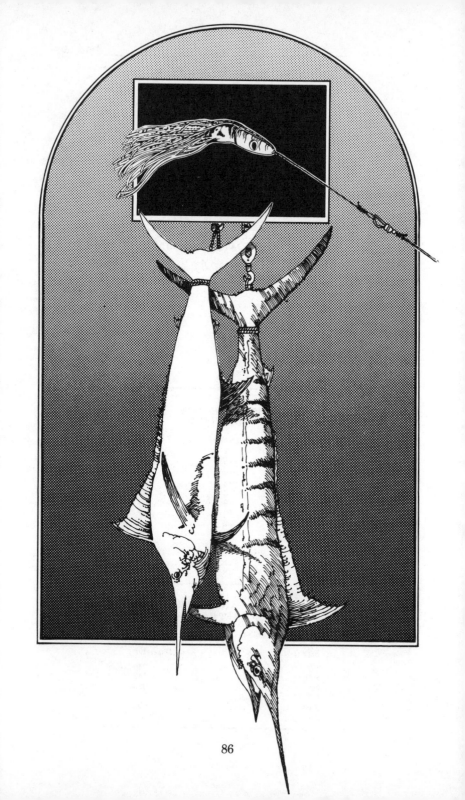

Chapter 3

Baits Rigs & Tackle

Leaders & Rigs

Tips on Leader Selection

Fishing leaders can be divided into two broad classifications:

1. Leaders designed for lowest possible visibility, so that lure or bait looks, to the fish, as if it isn't connected to anything.

2. Leaders designed to protect the line from shock, abrasion, sharp teeth, or from being cut by the fins or tail of exceptionally large fish.

The perfect leader would be one which is virtually invisible, yet strong enough to resist even the jaws of a mackerel or barracuda. Unfortunately, there is no kind of leader material which comes close to providing the advantages of both extremes; therefore, any leader you make up, for any kind of fishing, is necessarily compromised to some extent.

Low-visibility leaders are generally used in freshwater fishing, and in a few saltwater specialties, such as bonefishing. In fact, for the great majority of freshwater fishing the angler needs no leader at all, IF he is using monofilament line. The line serves as its own low-visibility leader, and nothing heavier is usually needed. However, the angler who uses braided line is advised to use a simple monofilament leader for reduced visibility, even if the breaking test is the same as that of his line. He can, of course, use either lighter or heavier mono as conditions dictate.

But there are many freshwater occasions when a monofilament leader heavier than the line is called for. Even the small teeth of a bass might wear through extremely light line (say 6-pound-test and under), and so the ultra-light angler may find it advisable to tie on a mono leader of around 12- or 15-pound-test in some instances. With lines of 8- to 15-pound-test (the usual size range for most freshwater fishing) it pays to employ a 20- or 30-pound-test monofilament leader when fishing in or near thick weeds. It's also a good idea to use the heavy leader when live-baiting for bass. Bass often swallow a bait deep, and if you hook the big one you're always hoping for, he just might manage to fray your 10- or 12-pound line before you can get him to the net.

All fly-fishing leaders, of course, fall into the low-visibility classification. A fly line is very thick, and so a monofilament leader must be used to form a less visible connection to the fly. Sometimes (mainly in salt water) additional protection is also needed at the fly, and this is accomplished through a heavy tippet, attached to the regular thin fly leader. Information on fly leaders of various kinds is given in a succeeding section.

Except when fishing for gar and larger members of the pike-pickerel clan, the freshwater angler is not apt to need a mono leader heavier than 30 pounds, or a wire leader. But leaders designed for protection, rather than low visibility, are necessary in just about every area of saltwater fishing.

MONOFILAMENT OR WIRE?

Monofilament leaders should get first call over wire in the great majority of applications. Use wire only in cases where monfilament is likely to fail—such as big-game fishing, or fishing for sharp-toothed species (mackerel, bluefish, barracuda, etc.).

Snapper, grouper and sea trout (weakfish) are a few examples of fish which possess formidable-looking teeth, yet they do not seriously threaten monofilament leaders because their teeth are not designed for shearing or clipping. Monofilament is a better choice than wire for any of those species.

A few species, though possessing no visible teeth, own exceptionally raspy or bony jaws. This group includes the tarpon and snook. Monofilament leaders can and should be used for both species (when casting, anyway), but it must be heavy enough to withstand the raspy jaws over a considerable length of time. Mono as heavy as 100-pound-test is needed when seeking large tarpon—say 75 pounds and heavier. For smaller tarpon, and for snook, 40- to 60-pound leaders are about right, while 30-pound-test is the minimum practical size, even for snook that average less than 10 pounds.

Why not use thinner wire, rather than thicker monofilament, for such fish as snapper, grouper, tarpon or snook? Because it seems obvious from the cumulative experience of many anglers that even the thinnest wire is more likely to spook a fish than is monofilament of considerably greater diameter. Also, the supple monofilament is not subject to some of the pitfalls that accompany the use of wire—kinking, spiralling, etc. And an important benefit for the caster is the fact that the soft mono allows much better action with almost every sort of artificial lure.

Wire is less objectionable when trolling than when casting—possibly because most fish approach a trolled bait from the rear, or possibly because the wake of the boat helps camouflage the leader.

CHOOSING WIRE MATERIAL

In those instances where wire leader is a necessity, the angler still must select between single-strand wire and cable or twisted wire. Another option is cable which has been coated with nylon.

Though single-strand wire is the most popular, there are no ready-made rules to help you in making your own selection. The only thing that can be done here is to discuss the merits and demerits of each, and mention a few popular applications.

Single-strand stainless leader wire is less expensive than cable. It also is faster and easier to secure, and is more readily adaptable to rigging a variety of baits. Thus, single-strand is the overwhelming choice of both charter boatmen and private anglers who do a lot of offshore fishing. It also is widely used (in smaller diameters) for inshore trolling.

The main disadvantage of single-strand wire is that it can kink and seriously weaken the leader. You must inspect it frequently for such kinks, and if any are observed, the kink must be cut out and the leader re-wrapped or replaced. Do not attempt to "unkink" the leader by bending it in the opposite direction, as this will weaken it even more. However, minor offset bends which develop in single-strand wire can safely be straightened without appreciable loss of strength.

Cable wire is more supple than single-strand, and so is a logical choice for casters who require a short wire leader. Nylon-covered cable is more supple yet, and you might prefer to use it instead of plain cable—however, sharp-toothed fish can quickly shred the soft coating, and so you may have to change leaders more often.

Heavy cable leaders are used in some big-game applications, particularly for the quest of extra-big marlin with heavy tackle. Cable is resistant to kink-breakage, which single-strand is not.

Another common use of heavy cable leader is in bottom-fishing for big tarpon on the Gulf Coast of Florida. Guides in that neck of the woods like to use a dead mullet bait, and let it rest on bottom.

Their aim also is to let the tarpon swallow this bait quite deep. This, of course, brings the leader into direct contact with the tarpon's strong mouth, and he is quite likely, during the ensuing fight, to bend single-strand wire to the breaking point. (The bait and rig for this type of fishing is illustrated in another section.)

Guides at Boca Grande on the Gulf Coast, however, fish their tarpon with live bait, deep, but not on bottom. They use heavy single-strand wire, and seldom experience leader breakage because their tarpon almost always are hooked in the forward portion of the upper jaw.

LEADER LENGTH AND CONNECTION

For all kinds of casting, the monofilament leader should be tied directly to your line, using the Surgeon's Knot or the Albright Special. Even for the lightest fishing, the mono leader should be at least two feet long. This allows a few inches of leader to be cranked inside the tip guide when you cast, and means that the leader—not the light line—will be absorbing the strain and chafe of the tip during the cast.

Much longer mono leaders are required for certain heavy-duty types of casting, such as surf-fishing and ocean-casting with lures weighing two ounces and up. Your mono must be long enough so that it will go through all the guides and wrap a couple of times around the reel—and still leave the necessary casting length outside the tip guide. This arrangement is sometimes referred to as a "shock line" or "shock leader."

As a matter of fact, this shock-leader arrangement is a good one to use as your *basic* leader rig for just about every kind of saltwater fishing with spinning tackle or light-line classes (under 30-pound-test) of general tackle. Here's how it works: Tie several feet of 30- or 40-pound-test monofilament directly to your line. Most of the time this will be all the leader necessary, and because you have a goodly length of it, you can change lures frequently, cutting the leader back a number of times before it gets so short you have to change it.

Now, if you get into mackerel, say, or bluefish, you simply add a short length of wire, 12-18 inches, to the end of your shock leader, using a small black swivel as a connector. If you want to go after big tarpon, tie 12 inches of 80- or 100-pound-test mono to your shock leader, using the Albright Special Knot. When you take a yen for bottom-fishing, slip your sinker onto the shock leader, then tie on a swivel and add the desired length and size of additional leader.

The long shock leader has numerous advantages, of which shock-absorption is only one. It acts as a safeguard against a large fish wrapping up in the leader and breaking the line; it guards against a big fish reaching past a short leader and breaking or cutting the line with his tail; it better takes the abrasive punishment of underwater obstacles, such as coral or oysters.

MONO LEADER SUGGESTIONS
(For lines of 20-pound-test and under)

Type of Fishing	Leader Length	Leader Test (Pounds)
Most freshwater	2–3'	none to 20
Bonefish, permit	2–3'	none to 15
All-around inshore	2' to rod length	30–40
Snook, tarpon	rod length	30–50
Deep jigging, reef bottom fishing	rod length	50–60
Ocean casting (surface and mid-depth)	rod length	30–60

NOTE: Add a short tippet of 80 or 100-pound mono *to your basic leader* when fishing for big tarpon. Add a short tippet of wire if likely to be getting strikes from bluefish, mackerel, kings, barracuda, shark. In either case, the tippet should be about 12 inches long.

WIRE LEADER SUGGESTIONS

Type of Fishing	Wire Length	Wire Size
Inshore spinning, trolling, drifting light bottom fishing	6" to 3'	2–5
Offshore trolling and drifting (all purpose)	6' to 10'	6–8
Offshore trolling (billfish, yellowfin tuna) with lines of 50-pound-test and under	12' to 15'	9–12
Offshore trolling (billfish, giant tuna) with lines over 50-pound	15' to 30'	10–19
Bottom fishing and deep reef trolling	3' to 9'	7–9
Jewfish Fishing	3' to 9'	9 and up
Shark fishing (large shark)	12' to 15'	9 and up

Leaders
for Heavy Tackle

Long wire   *Line*

Snap swivel

STANDARD OFFSHORE LEADER (WIRE)

To make line ready for instant attachment or change of leaders, first form the desired length of double line, then tie to the end of the double line a Pompanette or other type of heavy-duty snap swivel. The Improved Clinch Knot may be used to tie the swivel.

Prepare the wire leader by forming a small loop on one end, using the Haywire Twist, and attaching your hook or rigged bait to the other end, also with the Haywire Twist. Refer to the table of Wire Leader Suggestions for size and length of wire.

Several of these leaders can be made up in advance, coiled neatly, and kept ready for quick change simply by unsnapping and re-snapping the snap swivel.

You can either rig your baits to the leaders, as needed, or you can rig several baits in advance (leaders and all) and keep them coiled and ready in an ice chest.

You may, of course, use an ordinary swivel instead of a snap swivel. In this case, you would not make the wire loop, but merely leave the end of the leader as is, so it can be wrapped to the swivel.

Short wire · Long mono · Snap swivel

OFFSHORE LEADER—
WIRE AND MONOFILAMENT

Quite a few charter boatmen are now using heavy monofilament leaders for offshore trolling—with only 18-24 inches of wire at the end. The short length of wire is ample to guard against cutting by bill or teeth, and it also makes bait-rigging easier. Many rigged baits are difficult, if not impossible, to make with a monofilament leader.

This leader arrangement is especially helpful to anyone who fishes offshore in a small boat, or even a large boat with a cramped cockpit. The monofilament is much easier to control in tight quarters than is a long length of wire, and offers other advantages as well.

Again, start with a snap-swivel tied to your double line.

Prepare the monofilament leaders in advance. The monofilament will form all but a couple of feet of your overall leader and should test 80 or 100 pounds. Using the Improved Clinch Knot or the Two-Wrap Hangman's Knot, tie a stout swivel to one end of the leader; a Pompanette snap-swivel to the other.

The short wire tippets can also be prepared in advance, with or without baits. You rig as usual and form a wire loop in the other end, as usual.

Snap the monofilament leader to your line by attaching the *plain swivel* of the leader to the *snap-swivel* on your line. The wire is then attached to the *snap-swivel* at the other end of the monofilament leader.

Change baits simply by snapping the short wires on and off the monofilament. The heavy mono section of leader seldom needs changing.

OFFSHORE LEADER—
HEAVY WIRE CABLE

This leader is not illustrated because it consists simply of a single length of heavy cable, usually 15 to 30 feet, with a hook rigged to one end and a large swivel to the other. The sleeve-and-crimp method of attaching the hardware is explained in the section on Wire Wraps. Refer also to the general discussion on leaders at the beginning of this chapter, for more information on the cable leader.

Heavy cable is preferable to single-strand wire leaders for the following fishing specialties: giant marlin, giant swordfish, big sharks, big bottom fish at extreme depth (for instance, warsaw grouper), tarpon when using the Gulf Coast tarpon rig, or any bait which is likely to be swallowed deep by the tarpon.

Leaders
for Light Tackle

(Spin, Baitcasting, Surfcasting, Service Tackle)

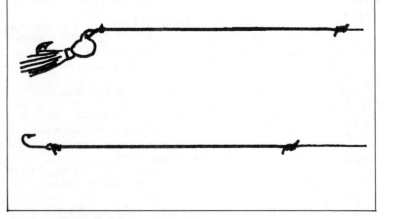

ALL-PURPOSE STRAIGHT MONOFILAMENT

This is the simplest of leaders and the most widely useful, consisting of nothing more than a length of heavy monofilament tied directly to your line.

For freshwater and light saltwater fishing, make the tie with the Surgeon's Knot.

For any kind of saltwater fishing where your line is apt to be put to the full test of its strength, make a double line first, then tie your leader to the double line, using the Albright Special Knot. Only with a double line can you be sure of getting 100 per cent knot strength.

As indicated by the two illustrations, most lures should be tied to the heavy mono with a Loop Knot. Hooks for fishing with bait should be tied with the Improved Clinch Knot.

Recommended *lengths* of mono leaders are discussed at the beginning of this chapter. Recommended *strengths* are shown in a separate table.

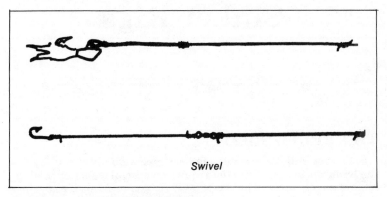

Swivel

MONO LEADER WITH HEAVY OR WIRE TIPPET

In some cases (as has already been discussed) it is desirable to add an additional short leader (called a tippet) to your basic leader.

You can add heavier mono by tying it on with the Albright Special Knot.

You can add light cable or nylon-coated cable, by tying it on with the Albright Special OR by swivel. The swivel should be tied to the leader with the Improved Clinch Knot. The wire tippet must be attached to the swivel by means of the Figure-Eight Knot or a crimped sleeve.

If you wish to add single-strand wire, a swivel is the best way. Be sure to use the Haywire Twist in wrapping your wire to the swivel.

STRAIGHT WIRE LEADERS

With lines under 20-pound-test, it is seldom advisable to use a straight wire leader without a shock leader of monofilament. Though you can often get by without it, the added strength of the shock leader is highly desirable.

However, if you wish to use a wire leader up to three or four feet long, without the shock leader, rig it as follows:

Wrap your wire to a swivel, using the Haywire Twist. Wrap the other end of the wire to your hook or lure, also by means of the Haywire.

If you desire fast lure or bait change, you can use the Quick-Change Wrap, which is quite dependable though not as strong as the Haywire.

Tie the leader to your line with the Improved Clinch Knot.

Sinker Rigs

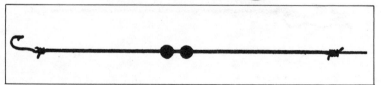

THE SPLIT-SHOT

Split-shot sinkers are the smallest type available—and by far the handiest to use. Split-shot require no special leader or rigging, but are merely pressed onto whatever rig you're using, if and when a small amount of weight is needed to improve casting ease, or to sink your bait a bit faster.

The split-shot has long been standard in freshwater fishing, but is largely overlooked by saltwater anglers. Yet it can be just as helpful to folks who fish the coast. The saltwater fisherman who keeps split-shot handy will find many instances when he is able to add just the right amount of added weight without having to re-rig with a different type of sinker—which likely as not is bigger than he really needs.

Press the split-shot to line or leader, using pliers. The shot is best positioned about six inches from the hook.

If more than one shot is used, do not place them close together, but keep them about an inch apart.

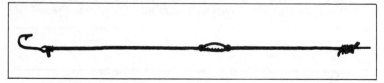

CLINCH-ON OR RUBBERCOR SINKER

The clinch-on is a tapered sinker, with a full-length groove and soft "ears" at either end. You attach the clinch-on simply by laying your line or leader in the groove of the sinker, folding the "ears" over the line, then pressing the groove closed with pliers.

The Rubbercor is a patented sinker, which works in much the same way as the clinch-on. But it is a much-improved design and considerably easier to use, because it can be taken off and put on at will—with no pliers and without bruising the line or leader.

Instead of the lead ears, the Rubbercor has a center insert of rubber, which protrudes at both ends of the sinker. You lay your line in the groove, twist the rubber ends and your line is secured. To remove, twist the rubber ends in the opposite direction.

Clinch-on and Rubbercor sinkers come in various weights, and are especially useful in weights of one-quarter ounce and heavier, where they replace several split-shot.

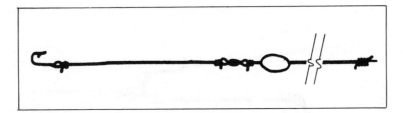

SLIDING OR EGG SINKER RIG

This is pretty much the standard sinker used for saltwater fishing. Egg sinkers range in size from one-quarter ounce to several ounces, but the basic rig shown here is widely used with all of them —whether you're using a half-ounce sinker on a spinning rod for inshore channel fishing, or a two-ounce sinker on a boat rod for reef bottom fishing.

First you slide the sinker onto your line (or shock leader); then tie on a swivel, using the Improved Clinch Knot; then add your leader and hook.

As you can see, the egg sinker is free to travel along your line, but is stopped well above your hook by the swivel. When a fish bites, he can take out line without feeling the weight of the sinker.

It is advisable to use a shock leader, or double line, above the swivel, because the free-running sinker often bangs hard against the swivel while you're fishing. If your light line is tied straight to the swivel, your knot might be quickly weakened and a breakoff can occur.

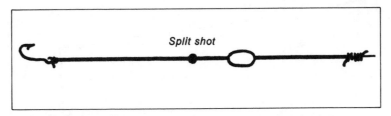

Split shot

EGG SINKER RIG WITHOUT SWIVEL

The egg sinker can be used without a swivel if you prefer.

If you're using a shock leader tied directly to a heavy tippet, simply slide the sinker onto your shock leader before you tie the tippet. The knot will be plenty large enough to assure that the sinker won't slide over it to your hook.

If you wish to use a shock leader without a heavy tippet, slide the egg sinker onto the leader before tying on your hook. Now, of course, it will be necessary to keep the sinker away from your hook because you don't have a swivel or a heavy-tippet knot to do it automatically. Just press a tiny split-shot to your leader at the desired point (at least a foot away from the hook) to keep the sinker from sliding farther.

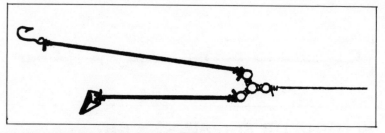

PYRAMID SINKER RIG

The egg sinker just doesn't hold position on soft bottom, if there is any current or wave action. That's why pyramid sinkers are the standard weights for surf and ocean-pier anglers.

The rig shown here is built around a three-way swivel: that is, a swivel with three eyes instead of the standard two. Tie your line or shock leader to one eye, using the Improved Clinch Knot. To the second eye, tie a short piece of heavy monofilament, and to the other end of the monofilament, tie your pyramid sinker. The Improved Clinch Knot serves for both ties.

The third eye, of course, is where you attach your leader hook and bait. Monofilament generally is the leader choice, but you might wish to use wire if expecting bluefish, shark, etc.

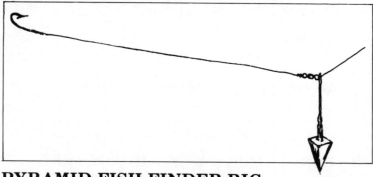

PYRAMID FISH FINDER RIG

The other basic rig for the pyramid sinker is the fish-finder or sliding-sinker arrangement. It works much like the egg sinker rig, in that the pyramid sinker is allowed to slide freely up and down the line or shock leader above your swivel.

This *could* be accomplished simply by threading your line through the eye of the pyramid sinker, but such an arrangement really isn't satisfactory. You should use a SINKER SLIDE, which can be purchased at most tackle stores in beach country.

The sinker slide is simply a small accessory which has an eye on one end (for your line to run through), and a snap on the other, to which your sinker is attached.

THE TROLLING SINKER

Trolling sinkers generally weigh several ounces and are used mostly with medium or heavy tackle, including wire line outfits, for deep-reef and ocean trolling.

Some trolling sinkers are torpedo-shaped, while others are kidney or keel-shaped. Some have a planing head which helps attain a greater depth. All have an eye at either end for ease of rigging.

Regardless of shape, they are all rigged as follows:

1. Tie a heavy-duty swivel to your line or double line.

2. Wrap about three feet of leader wire to the swivel, and wrap the other end of the wire to the forward eye of the trolling sinker.

3. Take a second length of leader wire, 3 to 6 feet long as desired. Wrap one end to the rear eye of the trolling sinker, and the other end to your hook or lure.

VARIATION FOR WIRE LINE: If using wire line, it is advisable to substitute heavy braided nylon line, at least 100-pound-test, for the wire mentioned in Step 2. This is a safeguard against the effects of electrolysis.

For this type of deep-trolling, you can use either a rigged bait (ballyhoo, mullet, strip, feather-strip), or else a large lure, such as a spoon or feather.

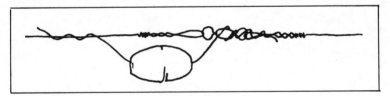

BREAKAWAY SINKERS

The obvious use of breakaway sinker rigs is to get your bait to the desired depth in situations which require so much weight that the sinker would be a disadvantage after a fish is hooked.

You can improvise a breakaway rig, using thread or light monofilament line, but the simplest and most effective method is to run a length of soft copper wire (such as you buy for rigging ballyhoo) twice through the eye of an egg sinker. This leaves some of the wire protruding from either end. Wrap one end *lightly* to the eye of your swivel; and wrap the other end around your leader with two or three wide spirals.

This will hold the sinker firmly enough in place so that you can drop it down. When a fish is hooked, the soft wire lets go usually on the first dash.

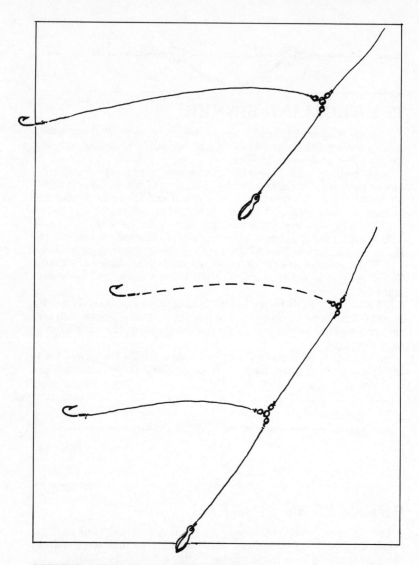

VERSATILE BOTTOM RIG

This is one of the most popular of bottom rigs, and can be used by varying the size of hook and sinker in virtually every area of saltwater fishing—in bays, from bridges and piers, in the surf, and in deepwater party boat angling. As you can see, it differs from the preceding pyramid sinker rig only in that a bank sinker (or other style) is used instead of the pyramid. Also, as the illustration shows, two or more three-way swivels may be incorporated into the leader for additional dropper lines with extra hooks.

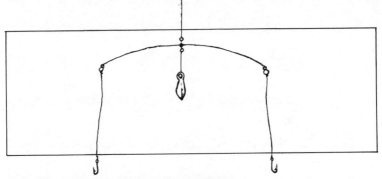

SPREADER BOTTOM RIG

Though used primarily for fluke and flounder fishing in bays, the spreader rig is a good one for fishing on any comparatively smooth bottom and for many types of fish.

While most anglers purchase them ready-rigged in tackle shops, it's not too difficult to fashion a spreader, using stiff, springy wire. Dropper lines for hooks and sinker are of monofilament. Your fishing line, of course, is tied to the swivel at the center of the spreader.

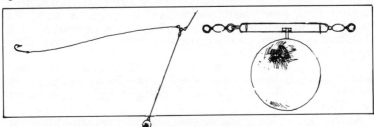

HEAVY BALL SINKER RIGS

Perfected in the San Francisco Bay area for getting baits down to striped bass when they are at depths which pretty much prohibit the usual rigs, heavy ball sinkers—sometimes weighing two pounds or more—are useful, too, in such specialties as plumbing extreme ocean depths for cod, snapper, grouper and tilefish.

One illustration shows the ball rigged to a three-way sinker as in preceding rigs with other types of weights. This would obviously require extremely heavy tackle and a lot of muscle to crank the ball back up, either with or without a fish attached. It's best used with a motorized reel.

The detailed drawing shows a device used in the Pacific northwest to release the ball once a fish is hooked, so the quarry can be fought on lighter tackle without the heavy weight. The sinker release is spring-loaded. You draw back the spring, insert the eye of the ball sinker into the aperture, and release the spring. When a bass or salmon hits, the spring is depressed and the sinker falls free. The sinker release is not used on a dropper line, but is simply tied into the leader by means of the swivels at each end.

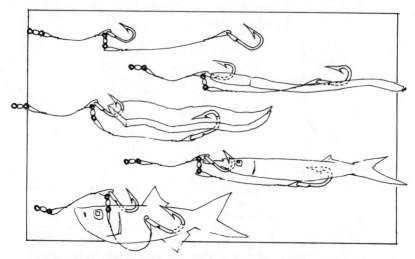

THE MANY-PURPOSE STINGER RIG

Here's a rig that can be used effectively with both live and dead natural baits, even plastic worms, and is a snap to make. It's called the "Stinger" because the trailing hook nips short-striking fish, or those which usually clip a bait in the middle and avoid a single, forward-placed hook.

The rig can be made with either monofilament or wire leader, and in a variety of hook sizes for such diverse purposes as swordfishing with whole squid and 14/0 hooks, and rigging a sandworm to 1/0 hooks.

All the illustrations show the connection between front and rear hooks made with a swivel. This is advantageous, since it allows the rear hook to be turned at will in any direction necessary for affixing it to the particular bait; however, the swivel may be eliminated and the connection made directly to the eye of the forward hook.

In rigging, when you run the leader through the eye of the forward hook, run it through the eye of the swivel before tying or wrapping off. Then take a separate short length of leader, tie or wrap it to the other eye of the swivel, and then wrap the second hook to the end of it.

Many anglers routinely use the Stinger Rig with live baits, whether they be kite-flown, drifted, slow-trolled or free-lined.

When used with dead baits, such as strips, ballyhoo, cigar minnows or squid, the front hook is inserted at the front of the bait, in the bottom and out the top, and the second hook placed wherever it happens to reach. The front hook now serves the same purpose as the "pin" in a regular trolling-bait rig.

When grass is a problem, you would not wish to use a Stinger Rig for trolling—but it *could* be done. And the Stinger is the best of all rigs for *drifting* dead baits.

Float Rigs

How do you select the proper size and type of float? Follow these guidelines:

Cane-pole fishermen should use a very small float, or one of the slender designs (many still like the old turkey quill) so a bream or perch can take it under without feeling much resistance.

Larger floats are for bigger baits and, hopefully, bigger fish. The design is not actually too important. Just try to use the smallest size which will support the bait you're using. This is especially important with live baits. You don't want a float which can be easily pulled under, and kept under for long periods, by your bait. It can be difficult to tell when the strike comes.

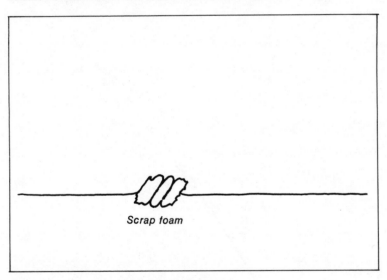

Scrap foam

THE BREAKAWAY FLOAT

When fishing with live bait offshore (or for big tarpon inshore), it is much more enjoyable and convenient if you use a float which breaks away after the fish is hooked.

Your float in this case is merely a chunk of scrap plastic foam. You should be able to obtain plenty of scrap material from broken and discarded foam ice chests. If not, you can buy blocks of foam in most dime stores.

All you need do is wrap your line several times around the chunk of foam at the desired depth. Pull on your line to make it bite into the soft plastic. It is quickly thrown when a fish is hooked.

FIXED FLOAT RIG

This is the standard setup for fishing with a float. The rig remains basically the same, although it can be used with a wide array of floats—in various sizes and designs.

The float is placed at a pre-determined depth, and fixed there so it will not move. The manner in which it is fixed, depends on the design of the float.

Many floats have a hollow center and a peg. You run the line through the center of the float and fix it in position by inserting the peg. Obviously, you must thread the float on your line *before* tying on your leader or hook.

Other floats have a spring-loaded clip. By simply pressing a button, you can affix or remove the float at will.

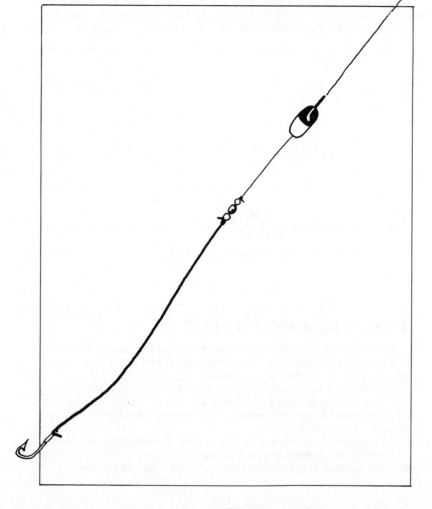

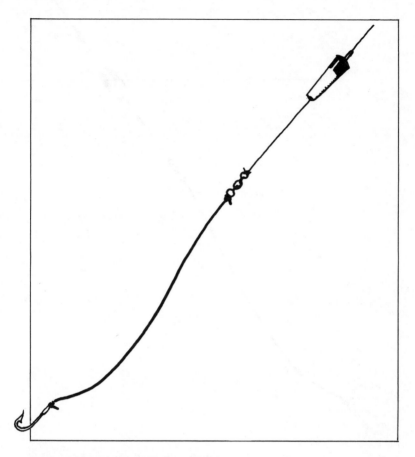

POPPING CORK RIG

This is the same as the fixed-float rig, the only difference being that you use a float which is specifically designed to pop the surface of the water when you twitch the tip of your rod.

Just like an ordinary float, the popping cork supports your bait at the desired depth, and signals a strike. But it also *helps attract fish to your bait*. Instead of letting the cork lie still, you pop it at frequent intervals (be sure to take up any slack line which results). The noise is attractive to many predatory fish. The popping cork is most widely used for trout, but can be equally deadly on redfish, snook, jack and other species.

Popping corks are identifiable by their wide, scooped-out heads. They are available in weighted and unweighted models.

The unweighted model floats on its side when at rest. It pops well only if you're using a sinker between the cork and your bait.

The weighted model has a bit of lead molded inside of it, and so rides the surface head-up. Use the weighted one if you're fishing with no sinker.

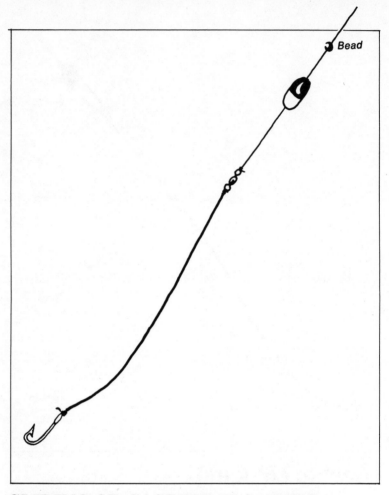

Bead

SLIDING OR CASTING FLOAT RIG

It can be awkward, or even impossible, to cast with a fixed float —especially if your float is several feet above the bait.

You want a float which slides right down to your swivel or sinker as you cast, yet stops at the desired depth after your bait hits the water.

To achieve this, you must use a sliding float in conjunction with a plastic, hollow bead.

First, tie a knot in your line at the point where you want the float to stop. Now thread the bead onto your line below the knot, then thread the float onto your line below the bead. Last, tie on your leader (or hook and sinker, if using no leader).

The hole in the bead is too small to permit passage of the knot, therefore the bead stops at the knot. And the bead, of course, stops the float. Beads can be purchased at tackle counters. If necessary you could use a small button instead of the bead.

CAUTION: The knot you tie to stop the bead, severely reduces the breaking strength of your line! Unless you're using quite heavy line, it pays to tie on a long length of monofilament shock leader, and to tie your stop-knot in that.

BALLOON FLOAT

One of the most versatile and easily-carried of floats is an ordinary toy balloon. A package of balloons can be tucked away in a corner of your tackle box, out of the way until one is needed.

A balloon can be inflated to whatever size is needed to support your particular bait. Make a single knot in the balloon's lip to hold inflation, then stretch the lip and tie it around your line or leader at the chosen depth. The fight of a husky fish generally will burst the balloon, so that there is no added pressure on your rod as you tussle.

Balloons make especially effective floats when you want to drift the bait far from boat, bridge or shore, as it is carried easily by wind and current.

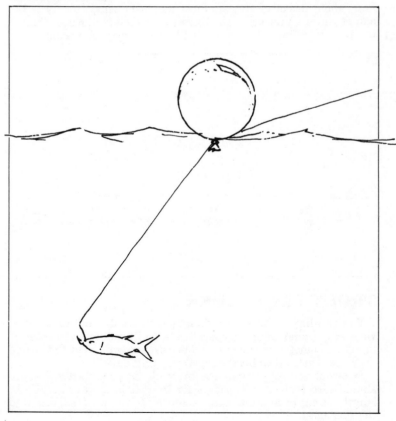

Fly Fishing Leaders

Most fly-fishing leaders are *tapered* leaders, built personally by the angler out of descendingly smaller diameters of monofilament leader material.

Tapered leaders cast much more efficiently than do level leaders. If properly matched to the fly (and if the mechanics of the cast are good) a tapered leader will always turn over neatly and deposit the fly at leader's length from the fly line.

When making tapered leaders, use the same brand of monofilament for all sections, since diameters may vary from brand to brand.

The sections may be tied together with either the Blood Knot or the Surgeon's Knot. When a heavy tippet is used, it usually is tied on with the Albright Special, although the Surgeon's Knot can be used.

First step in making tapered leaders is to tie a *permanent leader butt,* about 3 feet of 30-pound-test monofilament, directly to the end of your fly line, using the Uni-Knot or Fast Nail Knot. Though not really permanent, this butt will seldom need changing.

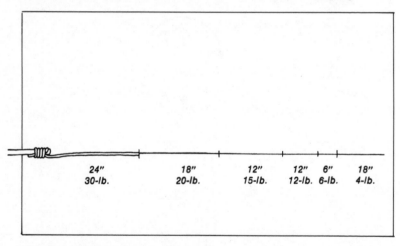

24"	18"	12"	12"	6"	18"
30-lb.	20-lb.	15-lb.	12-lb.	6-lb.	4-lb.

TROUT FLY LEADER

You can have a lot of fun fishing with small trout flies (dries, wets or nymphs) for panfish, such as bluegill, redbreast and stump-knocker. Sometimes you can clobber bream with trout flies when they are reluctant to hit the usual popping bugs.

For trout fishing you can use this leader as your starter. But you should also realize that leaders for trout fishing vary greatly in length, strength and makeup, according to the waters fished and the flies used.

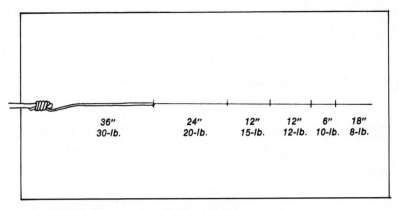

| 36" | 24" | 12" | 12" | 6" | 18" |
| 30-lb. | 20-lb. | 15-lb. | 12-lb. | 10-lb. | 8-lb. |

PANFISH-BASS LEADER

(Open water; small streamers or poppers)

This leader serves the same purposes as does the Level Leader described on Page 111, but will prove much more satisfactory than the level in the long run, and should be chosen by anyone who wishes to become a practiced and proficient caster.

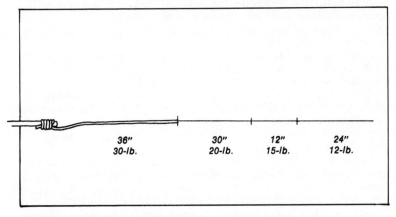

| 36" | 30" | 12" | 24" |
| 30-lb. | 20-lb. | 15-lb. | 12-lb. |

BASS OR SALTWATER LEADER

(Large streamers; large bugs)

This is the workhorse leader for inshore saltwater angling, as well as for bass fishing with big lures. Use it for trout, redfish, jack, many other types. For snook and small tarpon, you can add an additional one-foot Heavy Tippet of 40-pound-test monofilament. Tie this to the 12-pound material with the Albright Special or Surgeon's Knot.

For mackerel, barracuda or bluefish, you can add a one-foot Heavy Tippet of light wire cable, either plain or nylon-coated. Tie the cable to your 12-pound material with the Albright Special. Tie your fly to the cable with the Figure-Eight Knot.

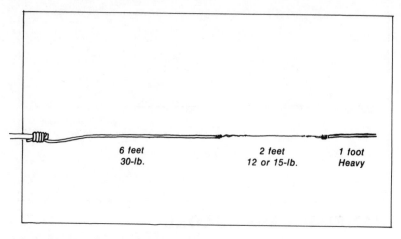

| 6 feet | 2 feet | 1 foot |
| 30-lb. | 12 or 15-lb. | Heavy |

HEAVY SALTWATER LEADER

This is the leader used for "big game" fishing with the saltwater fly rod—giant tarpon, shark and various offshore species such as kingfish, amberjack, blackfin tuna, sailfish and other huskies. (If you're fishing specifically for dolphin, you can safely use the general-purpose saltwater leader described earlier.)

The makeup of this leader is simple, but you must prepare it with considerable time and care.

First, use the Uni-Knot or Fast Nail Knot to tie on a leader butt of 30- or 40-pound-test monofilament, six feet long (slightly longer to allow for knot).

Second, take a piece of 12-pound or 15-pound-test monofilament, *six feet long,* and make a double-line in *both ends.* Tie one of the double-line ends to the leader butt, using the Albright Special. Tie the other double-line end to your Heavy Tippet, again using the Albright Special.

After you get through doubling both ends of your light material, and tying them to butt and Heavy Tippet, your section of light material will measure somewhere around two feet long. If it comes out longer, you're O.K. Nor is there anything to worry about if it comes out slightly shorter than two feet. But if it comes out shorter than one foot, redo it.

Your Heavy Tippet should be one-foot, no longer. If tarpon fishing, make your Heavy Tippet of 100-pound-test monofilament. If offshore or shark fishing, make it of cable, or nylon-coated cable.

Tournament, club and Salt Water Fly Rodders of America rules all require that the light material ahead of the Heavy Tippet be no less than 12 inches long.

The same rules require that the Heavy Tippet itself be no *longer* than 12 inches, and this measurement must include the knots.

If your Heavy Tippet is of stout monofilament, tie it to your fly with the Two-Wrap Hangman's Knot. If using cable, tie on your fly with the Figure-Eight Knot.

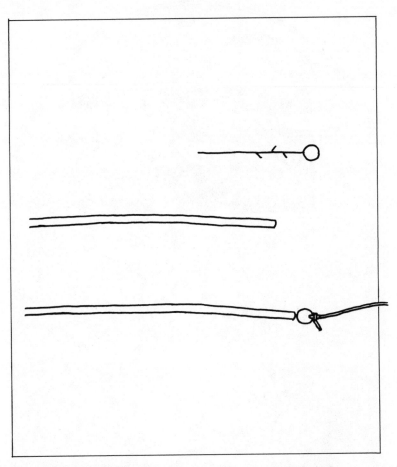

LEVEL LEADER, NO-KNOT EYELET

Though trout fishermen would shudder, the most common fly leader used by southern freshwater anglers is simply a level length of monofilament, usually in 6-, 8- or 10-lb.-test, and seldom any longer than 6 or 7 feet.

Panfish and average-size bass are not very sophisticated, so the short level leader normally does an adequate job, and it casts well enough with the popper and plastic molded insects, which are the main lures used.

Simplest method of attaching the level leader is to use a patented No-Knot Eyelet, which is sold in most tackle stores. This is nothing more than a barbed straight pin with an eye in the end of it. Push the barbed pin carefully into the hollow core of your fly line. Tie your leader to the eye, using the Improved Clinch Knot.

The No-Knot Eyelet is very strong and not apt to fail in freshwater fishing, if carefully installed.

111

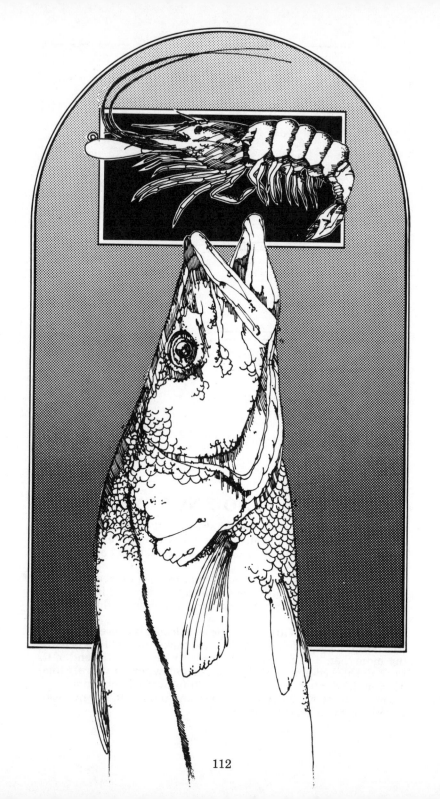

Chapter 4

Baits Rigs & Tackle

Baits & Lures
Freshwater Baits

LIVE BAITFISH

Live shiners, chubs and similar baitfish are the standard natural bait of bass fishermen everywhere. They can be purchased at all bait shops and fishing camps, but the ones you buy are generally commercial hatchery shiners and rather small—about three inches long on the average.

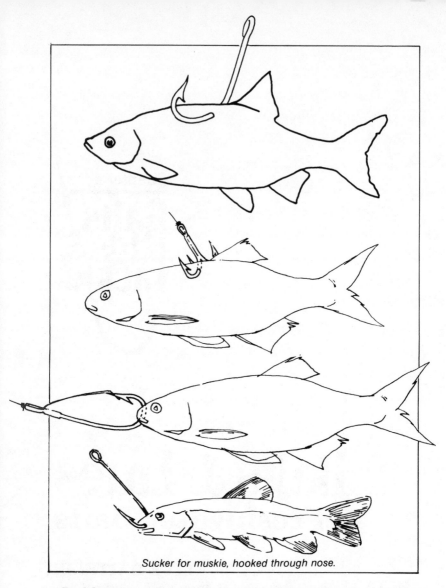

Sucker for muskie, hooked through nose.

Real bass specialists prefer to catch their own native shiners, using cane pole, light bobber and No. 10 hook with bread balls for bait. Liberal chumming with watered bread helps attract shiners to the bait.

Native shiners often run six or eight inches in length, and sometimes nine or 10 inches. They don't come too big to suit bass anglers who seek huge largemouths.

Naturally, more action can be expected with the small shiners, and some very big bass often hit little baits.

Smaller bait-store shiners should be used with about a 3/0 hook.

With big native shiners, tie on at least a 5/0 hook, and don't be afraid to use hooks as large as 8/0—preferably in a bronzed freshwater pattern.

When you're using a float rig, it's usually best to hook the shiner lightly through the dorsal surface. However, when drift-fishing or slow trolling (with a bobber or without) you'll get more natural swimming action by hooking through both lips.

In weedy areas, a large weedless hook can be used, and the lip hookup is best for this.

LIVE BREAM

Small bream (usually bluegill, but other species can be used too) make excellent baits for bass in states where legal.

As with shiners, larger bream are apt to lure bigger bass.

Hook bream exactly the same as described for shiners.

There's absolutely no doubt that shiners are much preferred for bass bait by fishermen in general. However, quite a few specialists use bream by choice. Note too that there will be times when shiners are scarce, but a few bream can almost always be taken by fishing with worms or bread balls.

LIVE MINNOWS

Probably three-fourths or better of all live minnows used in fresh-water fishing are dunked by anglers seeking crappie (speckled perch). But as the devout perch fisherman has learned long ago, minnows will take just about anything in sweet water—bream, warmouth, pickerel, white bass, striped bass, black bass, even catfish.

Occasionally a crappie fisherman will miss out on his primary target, but return to dock with a nifty string of bluegills or war-mouth—all caught on minnows. And stories are legion concerning perch fishermen who find an 8- or 10-pound bass wallowing around on the end of their cane-pole line.

Because of their flimsy size, it's difficult to hook minnows through the back without doing them serious injury—even with very light-wire hooks. Therefore, the standard hookup for small minnows is through both lips.

Use only the tiniest of split-shot sinkers when fishing a minnow. This is a fragile bait that can't carry around much weight.

Should you run out of live minnows, dead ones can often be used with success if you hook them through the lips, then twitch your pole or rod to make the dead bait move through the water.

116

LIVE FROGS

Everybody knows that live frogs are great bait for bass. Still, they are not used too often because of the difficulty in procuring and handling them in any quantity. Some anglers go to frogs as a last resort—only when other baits aren't working. Then they chase down a frog or two. More often than not, the frog produces action.

The frog can be hooked lightly through one leg. Frog skin is tough and the hook seldom pulls out. If presented with no sinker or other terminal tackle, the leg-hooked frog really kicks up a commotion and attracts fish. Another common hookup is through both lips, as with a shiner or minnow.

In a clear-water situation, where perhaps you can see bass—and they can see you—a leg-hooked frog, presented on a light monofilament line with no other terminal tackle, will draw a strike when all else fails.

Sometimes you'll encounter a great number of very small frogs on the bank of lake or river. These are easily caught and make fine bait for bream and little bass. Use No. 8 hooks on pole or light spinning tackle, and hook the frogs in exactly the same way as already described.

CRAWFISH

Many river and creek fishermen swear by crawfish—the larger specimens for bass, and the smaller ones for bream, Of course, lake fish will eat crawfish too, but this bait is at its best when allowed to drift along with the current of a stream.

The easiest way to get crawfish is with a light and dipnet at night along the shallow edges of a stream. They roam and feed at night and are easily spotted with a light. You can get some in the daytime by turning over rocks and limbs in shallow water or small pools. Watch out for the pinchers—they smart, but do no serious damage to your fingers.

Like live shrimp in salt water, crawfish can be hooked lightly through the top of their hard forward shell (carapace). Most anglers, however, prefer to hook them through the tail as shown in the illustration. This helps a lot in keeping the crawfish from backing under a rock or root.

Toss the crawfish upstream, using a sinker just heavy enough to get you down near bottom. Let the current carry the bait downstream.

You may remove the claws without harming the bait's appeal, but folks who use crawfish often quickly learn to handle them and hook them up without getting pinched.

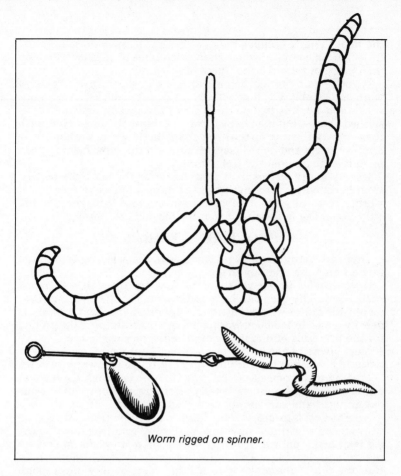

Worm rigged on spinner.

EARTHWORMS

From tiny red wigglers to huge "pond worms" and night crawlers, earthworms have been used by more freshwater fishermen than all other baits combined. And so it probably always will be, because worms just catch fish.

There are many ways of hooking worms, but the one illustrated is no doubt the best for bream and bass. Hook once through the center section, then turn the hook and go through the center section once more. If the bend of your hook is large enough, go through a third time.

This leaves both long ends of the worm free to wave around in the water—and the action attracts bass and those big bream just as much as whatever smell and taste appeal the worm might have. Seldom do you miss hooking a fat bream. Little ones will sometimes grab the end of a free-waving worm, but you don't want those anyway.

Kids, of course, often use a small piece of worm and thread it on the hook. That's because they don't want to miss those nibbling little fish. Of course, if you wish to catch some little fellows for bait, then you can thread a tiny piece of worm too.

If you're going for catfish or carp, you'll want to use a "gob" of worms. Probably you'll select a No. 1 or 1/0 hook. Start with one worm and hook it two or three times through the middle as described above—but then hook it two or three more times. Now push the worm all the way up the hook shank to the eye of the hook; take another worm and hook it several times in the same fashion, then push it close against the first worm.

Use as many worms as it takes to cover the hook completely, from barb to eye, with just what the name implies—a real gob of worms. Naturally, the number of worms needed to make a gob will vary according to the size of your worms and the size of your hook.

PROCURING WORMS

There are many ways to get worms—the easiest way being to go into a bait store and buy them.

If you prefer to dig your worms, look for them in soft, moist earth. Generally they can be found near a spring or well, or near an outside faucet where the ground stays wet. If no water source is nearby, you can tell good worm territory by examining the ground for the tiny hills of dirt that worms leave on the surface.

Most lawns in good condition are excellent worm territory. But naturally you don't go around digging up your lawn, or a lawn belonging to anyone else. What you CAN do is search the lawn at night with a flashlight, especially after a rain. Worms often come out at night and can simply be picked up.

Another way to get worms from a lawn (or from other good worm territory without having to dig) is by "grunting them." Your leg isn't being pulled! Grunting works. Drive a wooden stake into the ground, leaving a couple inches exposed above the surface. Rub the top of the stake with a large rasp, or any other rough metallic object that gives a good grating effect. Vibrations set off by this grunting drive the worms (if any are within range of the vibrations) to the surface.

CRICKETS AND GRASSHOPPERS

While crickets are selected as bait far more often than grasshoppers—for the simple reason they are widely sold in bait shops while grasshoppers are not—both insects are effective fish producers, and both are fished in the same way.

Both should be hooked through the thorax, which is the forward, crusty half of the body. The rear portion is soft and tears loose easily. You can run the hook in one side of the thorax and out the other, or else (as in the illustration), run the hook through from top to bottom.

There is no way to hook a cricket or grasshopper so that it will stay alive for any great length of time. But when hooked through the thorax they stay alive a reasonable period. Besides, when fished beneath the surface, a dead cricket is just as effective as a live one.

Most people do fish their crickets below the surface—using a small hook, split shot, and a very light cork or bobber. An excellent method, particularly in rivers and creeks, is to present the cricket with no terminal tackle of any kind except the light hook. It will float along, kicking at the surface for a while, then will begin to settle slowly. Big bream seldom can resist such a natural presentation, and they may strike anywhere from the surface to the deepest depth the unweighted cricket can attain.

Crickets and grasshoppers are widely considered to be the leading stream baits for bream, but they do work in lakes and ponds too.

As mentioned, crickets are sold at most bait stores. You can catch your own—but don't depend on catching enough bait the same day you plan to fish. It's much better to set aside an afternoon, catch your crickets, and keep them until the day of your trip. They will stay healthy and happy indefinitely in any mesh box or cage, with a few potato peelings for them to feed on.

Commercially-raised crickets, the kind sold at bait counters, are light in color and referred to as grey crickets. The ones you catch in the wild will be somewhat larger and much darker, deep brown or

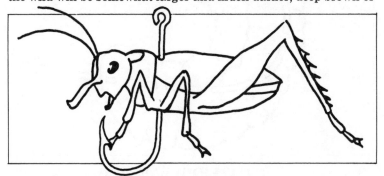

black. Regardless of color or species or size, they all seem to produce equally well.

Look for wild crickets in pastures or open fields, especially those liberally strewn with fallen limbs and other things the crickets can hide under. Turn over limbs, debris—anything crickets might hide under. They almost always stay hidden during the day.

While you hunt for crickets, you'll kick up grasshoppers from grass and low brush. Catch them if you like, for they make just as good an offering to the fish. However, catching grasshoppers requires more effort, since they often must be chased. Crickets don't move nearly as fast, or in such long hops.

Certain lighted areas attract crickets at night. Try, for instance, a lighted shopping center after closing hours (be careful the security guards or police don't call for the padded wagon). You can make the rounds of many lighted areas at the edge of town, near open fields or lots, and probably discover one or more places where crickets congregate. If you do, you'll have a dependable source of bait.

Insect Larvae

A great many common insects undergo a metamorphosis: that is, a change from one form to another during their life cycle. These insects begin life in a worm-like stage and are called larvae. Next they go into a dormant or pupal stage, during which they change into adult form. Well-known examples of larvae are the various caterpillars, which become moths and butterflies; and grubs, which become beetles.

So much for the lesson on entomology. The point for fishermen is that many, many types of larvae make excellent bait. Some larvae are commonly sold in bait shops; others are not, but can easily be obtained in the right place and right season.

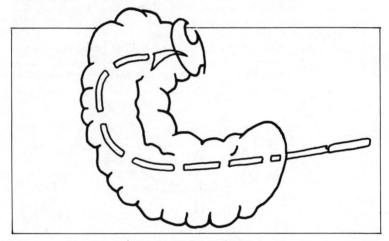

CATERPILLARS

Fishermen generally refer to fish-bait caterpillars as "worms," and identify the various species to their satisfaction simply by tacking on the name of the tree on which the worm is found: for instance, "catalpa worm," "oak worm," "camphor worm."

The catalpa worm is by far the most widely popular of bait caterpillars, and not a few fishermen keep catalpa trees for the sole purpose of raising a yearly crop of good bream bait. When small, catalpa worms are used whole on the hook. When they get big (and they do get *real* big) they are often broken in half, and sometimes turned inside-out before going on the hook—not a procedure for the queasy, obviously, but darn good bait.

Oak worms appear in great number on small oak trees, notably the black-jack oak, in early fall. Camphor trees get their crop of bait worms in late summer. Of course, these seasons vary slightly from area to area.

Actually, just about any kind of caterpillar makes good bait, although the three named are the most popular. There are exceptions, of course, and they can be painful exceptions. Shy away from stinging kinds, such as the saddle-back caterpillar, and all species which are covered with fuzz. Some very good bait species, however (including the oak worm), have small bristles which are harmless.

When small caterpillars are used for bait, they can be threaded on your hook as the illustration shows. Larger ones should be hooked once or twice at the tail end. If the skin of the caterpillar is tough, bring the point and barb of the hook outside the skin for easier hooking of the fish.

GRUBS

Most insect larvae referred to as "grubs" or "grub worms" are white or yellowish in color and have prominent hard heads with visible mandibles or pinchers. The majority are larvae of various beetles, and are found either in soft ground or under the bark of trees—usually dead trees but sometimes, as in the case of pine, in living trees as well.

Those aforementioned pinchers can indeed pinch. But you can safely use the bait simply by keeping your fingers away from the business end. One type of grub is called "sawyer." You'll sometimes find a rotting pine log in the woods so full of sawyers that you can hear them grinding away from several feet. Their noise sounds like sawing, hence the name. Sawyers are excellent bream baits.

Most grubs are small and should be threaded onto the hook as in the illustration.

BONNET WORMS

Actually, bonnet worms are caterpillars and should perhaps have been included in that category. But most fishermen don't *think* of them as caterpillars because of their habitat. They are found in the stems of bonnets, or lily pads, right out in the water. Look for pads which have a visible hole in the stem, right in the center of the pad. Pull up the stem and slit it carefully, and you'll find the worm (unless, of course, it has attained adulthood and departed). An awful lot of bream fishermen say bonnet worms are the very best baits of all.

SAND MAGGOTS

Sand maggots are one of the few larvae to be widely found in bait stores. The name sounds unappetizing, but the creature is far less repulsive than its title suggests. It is, in fact, cleaner and easier to use than most other larvae baits. Sand maggots are the larvae of the mole-cricket, and can be dug from sandy shores of some lakes. However, you'll find sand maggots far easier to buy than to procure yourself.

Other commercially-sold grubs include those called meal worms and golden grubs.

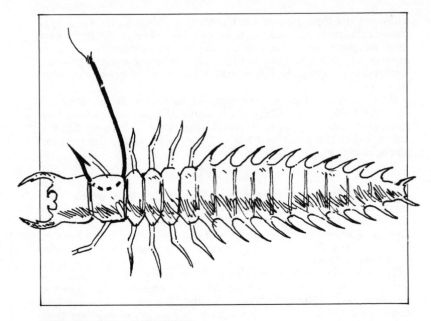

HELLGRAMMITE

Hellgrammites are the larvae of dobson flies and rank among the best all-around baits for river fishing, inasmuch as they are greedily snapped up by bass, trout and a variety of panfish. They are tough to corral, but can be taken by overturning logs and driftwood in slow-moving sections of streams. Careful—they can nip painfully. They are best fished by hooking once through the segmented body near the tail, then bumping them with the current along the bottom. In some areas of the south, hellgrammites are called "Gator fleas," and a few folks still believe that the hellgrammite goes out and catches the fish, instead of vice versa. This myth developed because the hellgrammite does indeed latch onto a fish which bites it, and occasionally a panfish will be landed even when the hook pulls free—because the "flea" hangs on.

GRASS SHRIMP

Small shrimp inhabit many fresh waters and are commonly called "grass shrimp." Many bait stores carry them, and if you know your waters you can dip-net or seine them from grassy areas.

Grass shrimp are small and it often takes two or three to make a suitable bait, even on a small bream hook. The illustration is deliberately magnified in effect, so you can see how several grass shrimp should be hooked at one time. Of course, any larger specimens you might find in your bait supply can be used singly.

Like saltwater shrimp, grass shrimp can be kept alive for a long time without being kept in water. They should be kept in a cold

124

container, moist, but protected from actually sitting in water. You can keep them in a can, or a waxed paper cup which, in turn, is placed in your portable ice chest.

If you don't carry an ice chest, keep them in a can on a bed of moist weed, cloth or newspaper.

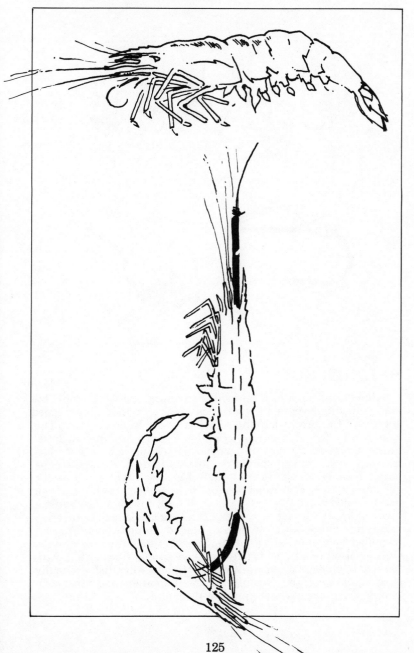

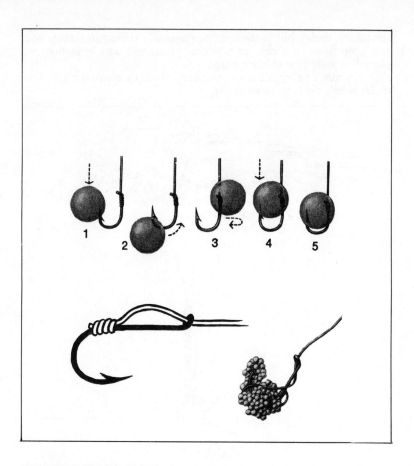

SALMON EGGS

Salmon eggs are a natural food of trout and are taken avidly by many other fish—including varieties which never see salmon eggs, except for the processed kind which are sold in jars as bait. The eggs can be fished singly or in globs. A single egg obviously requires a very small hook and a careful hookup, such as that illustrated above. The egg should be allowed to drift as naturally as possible along bottom in imitation of an egg swept along by the current. Globs of eggs must be aided in staying on the hook. If you use a snelled hook, then push the snell knot down on the shank, a bulge of line is formed. A portion of the egg cluster can be inserted under this bulge, which is then tightened. Or additional line can be pulled from above the knot and looped around the hook and the cluster. Another method is to tie the eggs in very fine netting. Artificial salmon eggs often work very well, and when fish are really gorging on eggs, they readily hit small spinners and other artificials which are colored orange or deep pink.

CATFISH BAITS

Since catfish will bite just about anything, it's surprising to see how many catfishermen go to the trouble of preparing special baits made out of blood, or smelly cheese or other unsavory substances. But they do catch catfish, and so you can't argue with them.

Many catfish enthusiasts keep their frying pans well supplied and never use any bait other than plain old earthworms (see the category headed "Earthworms" for instructions on making a catfish worm-gob).

Cats also will happily bite any of the other bream baits mentioned in these pages, and channel cats seem to show a special fondness for fat caterpillars.

Perhaps one reason so many catfishermen use special baits is that they don't want to be bothered by bream—especially the small bait-stealers.

If you want bait particularly for catfish, but don't wish to go in for special preparations, you can hardly do better than to slice up some beef or pork liver. For that matter, any kind of liver works.

Another popular catfish bait is a piece of frozen shrimp. Chunks of cut bait, from any kind of fish you can get your hands on, are also fine catfish producers, and are probably the most-used baits on trot lines.

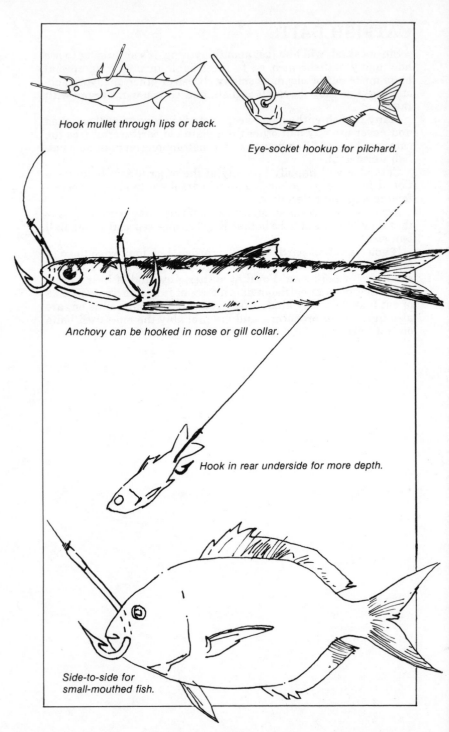

Hook mullet through lips or back.

Eye-socket hookup for pilchard.

Anchovy can be hooked in nose or gill collar.

Hook in rear underside for more depth.

Side-to-side for small-mouthed fish.

Saltwater Baits

LIVE FISH

Every coastal area has its popular types of live baitfish—anchovy, menhaden (mossbunker), mullet, sardine, shiner, spot, grunt, pinfish, cigar minnow, chub, mummichog, blue runner and goggleye, to name just a few examples.

When you get right down to it, virtually any small fish of appropriate size can be used for live bait.

Live catfish, for instance, makes an excellent bait for cobia, tarpon and snook. And stomach samples of deepsea fishes—from billfish to bottom feeders—prove they regularly eat such oddities as porcupine fish, trunk fish, file fish, etc.

The whole point is this: use the popular baits whenever possible —after all, they're proven. But if you can't get the desired species of baitfish, don't hesitate to put out any small fish you can come up with. Chances are, the fish care less than you do.

Placement of the hook in a live bait is important and can vary according to the species of baitfish and how you want it to act.

The two hook positions in the mullet illustrated above are common ones, used with many different types of fish. One hook is through both lips; the other through the back.

Use the lip hookup when slow-trolling, or any time when boat motion or current would tend to pull a back-hooked bait through the water sideways, or in an unnatural way.

Some anglers feel that small-mouthed baitfish, such as mullet or pinfish, should not be hooked through both lips for fear of impairing "breathing" ability and shortening bait life. Mullet often are hooked by inserting the hook point into the mouth, then upward through the top lip only. Bait such as pinfish or spot may be hooked from side to side just back of the jaws.

The back hookup generally is a better placement, since a striking fish is more apt to get the hook on its initial hit. So hook through the back whenever it allows you to present the bait so that it swims in a free and natural manner. Placing the hook forward in the back tends to keep the bait nearer the surface. Hook it toward the tail if you want it to swim downward.

Placing the hook just behind the anal fin, on the bottom of the baitfish, above, is best of all for trying to urge the bait down deep.

Hook placement in other portions of the bait's anatomy may be necessary because of the nature of the species. Shown above are the two hookups most commonly used by California anglers with live anchovies. The hook can be stuck through either the tough "nose" of the fish, or through the bony "collar" just aft of the gills.

Similarly, some other fish that are variously labelled sardines or pilchards may be too soft-fleshed to permit a reliable hookup through either the dorsal or the lips. A solution, as illustrated, is to run the hook through the eye socket, just above the eye.

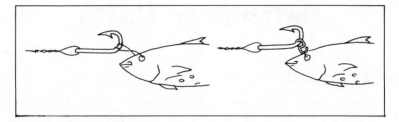

RIGGING LIVE BONITO

A live bonito probably is the best of all baits for offshore trolling —small ones measuring a foot or less for sailfish, etc., with tackle up to 50-pound-test; and larger live bonito for big marlin on heavy tackle.

Since live bonito of any size are often hard to procure, and because they don't live long in the average bait well, they usually are picked up individually on a small trolling feather and put to use at once.

In the interest of speed (when you aren't prepared in advance for a better hookup) hook your bonito through the lips and troll it slowly.

Properly, however, you should have a bait-needle ready, threaded with about 6 inches of nylon or Dacron line (20- or 30-pound-test). When the bonito comes aboard, have someone hold him firmly but gently with wet gloves, while you run the needle through the eye socket at about the 10 o'clock position. Remove the needle and quickly tie the ends of the line together to make a circle. The Surgeon's Knot, or simply a couple of overhand knots will do the job.

Now tie the circle of line in the middle, thus forming a figure-eight. Take the free end of the figure-eight and hitch it two or three times around your hook. The bait is ready to use.

If you're a serious marlin fisherman and want the best possible live bonito rig, get some pre-formed figure-eights made of brass. These are sold in most hardware stores (they're used as connectors for light chain).

To rig the metal figure-eight, use the bait-needle as before to thread a line through the bonito's eye socket. Tie the line tightly to one loop of the figure-eight, as close as possible to the bonito's head. Now you simply fix the other loop of the figure-eight over the bend of your hook. Obviously, when buying the figure-eights, you must be sure they are large enough to fit your chosen hook.

The metal figure-eight, because it is not bound tightly to the hook, allows the bait much more freedom of action. With this rig you can troll at your normal speed for dead-bait trolling—thus you do not have to retire your dead-bait lines using a live bonito.

Speed is of the utmost importance in getting a live bonito on the hook and back in the water. You should be able to rig in a few seconds, so practice rigging on dead baits until you can do the job efficiently but quickly.

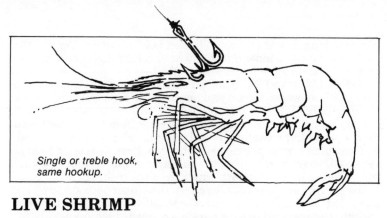

Single or treble hook, same hookup.

LIVE SHRIMP

King of live baits for coastal fishing is the live shrimp. It will take anything from bottom feeders to tarpon and king mackerel.

These are the two basic hookups for a live shrimp:

1. Atop the shrimp's head, you'll notice a horny ridge. Run the point of your hook lightly under this ridge, and out the opposite side.

2. Thread the shrimp onto your hook by inserting the point on the underside of the tail, then working it the full length of the tail section and out in back of the head.

System No. 1 allows the shrimp to move about freely. It is valuable.in situations where fish are extremely selective. The obvious disadvantage is that the hookup is flimsy. This means the bait is easily stolen by smaller fish. Still, you must use this hookup whenever it appears the fish are insisting on the most natural, free-swimming presentation.

System No. 2—the threaded shrimp—is considerably more durable and equally productive in many kinds of fishing. A lot of anglers use the flimsy head hookup when it really isn't necessary, thus wasting much expensive bait.

The threaded shrimp is entirely satisfactory for trout, redfish, bonefish, most snapper, grouper and many other species. Your shrimp should be threaded when using the popping cork (which see), because a head-hooked shrimp can be popped right off your hook. And, of course, the threaded bait is given plenty of action by your popping motions.

If a threaded shrimp works so well, why not use dead bait instead of live? Well, sometimes you can, and get good results. But experienced anglers know that the more desirable species of fish somehow prefer a shrimp with live appearance, smell and taste, over a dead shrimp—even though the live one may not be moving about.

KEEPING LIVE SHRIMP

A good live well, with re-circulating water or an aerator, is the most satisfactory repository for live shrimp.

Bait buckets with a removable perforated inner container work quite well. The inner container is kept on a line in the water while you're fishing. If you move, the bucket is filled with water and the container placed inside. But if you have a long distance to travel, be sure to change the water frequently.

THE ICING SYSTEM is an excellent one and will keep shrimp alive, without water, for several hours—even for a full day or more if you're careful. Here's how it works:

The shrimp must be transferred directly from the dealer's well into a water-tight container—a large waxed paper cup, an old coffee can, or even a plastic bag. This container then must be kept very cold, in an ice chest, but the shrimp must, at all times, be kept from coming in contact with water from the melting ice.

The colder you keep your ice chest, the longer your shrimp stay alive. It's best to have a separate small ice chest just for your shrimp. General-purpose ice chests are opened too frequently for drinks, etc., and this brings up the inside temperature.

CAUTION: Don't transport your shrimp on ice, then remove them and place them in a live well. If you use the icing method, stick with it all the way.

LIVE BLUE CRAB

The live blue crab is a preferred bait for permit fishing and the standard bait for tarpon fishing at Boca Grande. It also works well on many other fish, including snapper, grouper, snook and redfish.

"Dollar crabs"—that is, crabs approximating the size of a silver dollar—are the choice for both permit and tarpon. Tarpon will take larger crabs, but seem to favor the smaller ones.

Large live crabs make an excellent bait for deep bottom fishing for snapper and grouper. Let's say you've been fishing a deep hole or wreck where you can't avoid hooking amberjack every time you drop a live fish, or even a strip. You want to get past the amberjacks and try for a big snapper or grouper. The live crab is your solution. Amberjack won't touch it, yet the bottom fish love it.

No matter what size crab you use, remove the claws (for your personal safety), and hook as shown through the tip of the shell.

Crabs are easy to keep alive, either in a bait well or simply in a cool, damp place—such as a wet burlap sack.

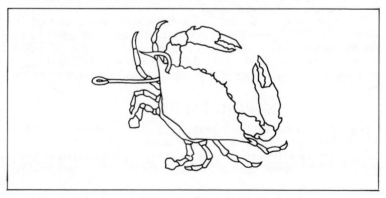

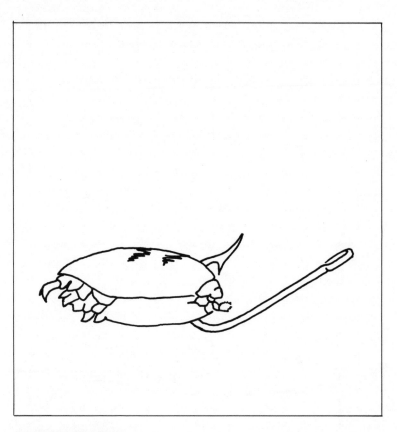

SAND FLEA

The sand flea is a specialized bait, used almost exclusively by surf and ocean-pier fishermen for pompano. It will take other surf species as well, but is unsurpassed as a pompano bait along beaches.

Sand fleas (not really fleas, but crustaceans) are sold at many beachside tackle shops, or they can be caught by the angler. Look for them at the edge of the surf where waves roll up on the sand, and then recede. As the wave recedes, look for V-shaped wakes in the soupy sand, made by the protruding antennae of the sand flea.

You must immediately scoop them out by digging under the "V" with your hand, to bring up a handful of sand which, you hope, has the sand flea in the middle of it.

Pompano specialists build a special scoop, which can be compared to a shovel with a wire-mesh bottom. They spot the antennae; dig out a big scoopful of sand; then let the sand filter through the mesh, leaving the fleas. Sometimes they get several baits at one scoop.

Hook the sand flea as shown in the illustration—once through from bottom to top.

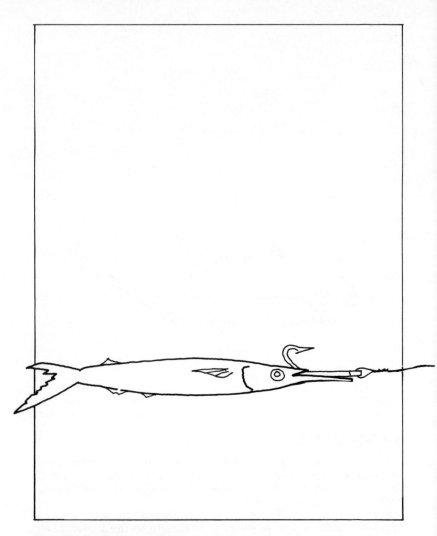

CATCHING AND FISHING
LIVE BALLYHOO

Ballyhoo, also called balao or halfbeak, has been employed for many years by ocean anglers as a standard dead bait. It is rigged whole for trolling, or is cut into strips and chunks.

In recent years, anglers have discovered that ballyhoo also make one of the premier live baits for many varieties of offshore game fish, and are well worth the effort it takes to catch them. Live ballyhoo are never found in bait shops because of the difficulty of keeping them alive and in good condition for any length of time.

While live-ballyhoo angling was developed in the Florida Keys and is still centered there, opportunities to catch and use these splendid baitfish exist in many warm waters of the world—in the Bahamas, throughout the Caribbean and tropical Latin America, and in many areas of the Pacific.

When disturbed, ballyhoo skitter across the surface of the water somewhat like flying fish, and this is how anglers often find them. Once skittering ballyhoo are located, the boat is anchored and a chum line begun. Ballyhoo respond readily to standard chums made from ground fish, and can also be chummed up with oatmeal or cracker crumbs. They stay at the top and can be spotted dimpling the surface of the water in the chum line. Once ballyhoo are near the boat, they can be caught by using very light line—no more than 10-pound test—to which is tied a No. 10 or No. 12 hair hook. The bait can be a tiny bit of cut fish or cut shrimp. Though an old-fashioned fishing pole makes the best ballyhoo-angling tool, few salty anglers are so equipped and most use light spinning rods (some do, however, keep telescoping glass poles aboard just for ballyhoo).

Regardless of what tackle is used, the bait must be drifted at the surface or just under it, and kept in sight by the angler so he can see the ballyhoo take the bait. Otherwise, he would not catch any, as ballyhoo do not deliver smashing strikes.

Even though it might be possible to catch a lot of them, you should resist the impulse to load up the baitwell with more than it can accommodate. Large stern-mounted wells on cabin cruisers can keep two or three dozen baits alive over a fishing day, but wells on small boats often cannot effectively keep more than a half-dozen.

When trolled for sailfish and other offshore species, a live ballyhoo should be pulled at just above idle speed. This is probably the slowest pace used for any bait. Ballyhoo also can be free-drifted or used on a kite. For that matter, many good fish are caught simply by drifting out a live ballyhoo on the very spot where you are catching the bait.

Ballyhoo belong to the group of fishes known as halfbeaks, and when you get your first close look at one it will surprise you to see that the "bill" is not an extension of the upper jaw but of the lower one. This curious physiognomy is the key to how you hook them.

Insert the hook into the mouth, point upward, and bring it out the top of the upper jaw. A small hook should be used, as a large one not only would tear out easily but would also diminish the action of the bait. Usual sizes are from 3/0 to 7/0, and in a rather light-wire hook, or a short-shank live-bait hook.

The mouth hookup described is the proper one for trolling, drifting, or for free-lining the ballyhoo in a current.

For kite-fishing, or for free-lining when current is not a problem, you may prefer to hook the ballyhoo through the dorsal surface near the midway point—taking care not to injure the spine.

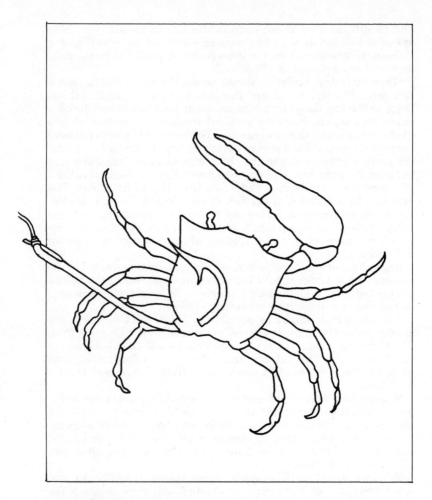

FIDDLER CRAB

A traditional bait for sheepshead, the fiddler crab can be found almost everywhere in tidal areas (though abundance varies with season). Besides sheepshead, fiddlers take snapper, redfish, grouper, drum—even an occasional snook.

You may find fiddlers on sandy shores, mud flats, or among mangrove roots. Sometimes they're in bunches that resemble waves moving across the sand. Unless they reach their holes, they are easy to chase and capture by hand.

Do not fear the one overgrown claw which gives the fiddler its name. Though it looks wicked indeed, it has little strength. The pinch of a fiddler crab can't break the skin, or even cause enough pain to make you say "Ouch."

To bait up with a fiddler, run your hook in at the base of any leg, and out anywhere along under the shell.

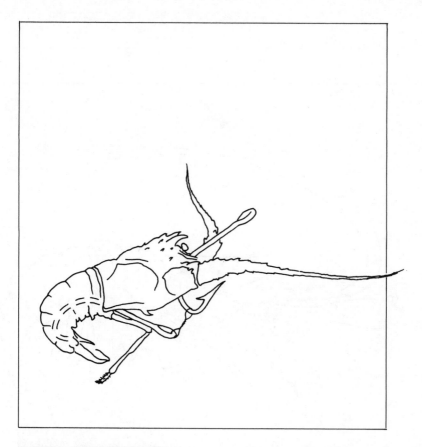

LIVE CRAWFISH

A live crawfish of legal size makes a mouthful of bait indeed. As you can guess, it's used only for big fish—giant cubera snapper, mainly, along the lower east coast of Florida and the Keys. Occasionally, the live crawfish is chosen as a bait for jewfish or big grouper.

Baby crawfish would be good bait for many fish, but it is unlawful to use them in Florida waters.

Obviously, the crawfish referred to is the saltwater variety, also called Florida lobster.

The double-hook rig shown here is the most satisfactory for cubera snapper fishing. Use two heavy-duty hooks, at least 9/0 and usually larger, and wire them together with cable and sleeves (see the section on wire wraps for instructions on securing the cable). The hooks are about four or five inches apart.

As the illustration shows, the upper hook goes between the "horns" of the crawfish. The lower one is inserted into the soft underside of the tail section, and out again.

Always handle live crawfish with gloves.

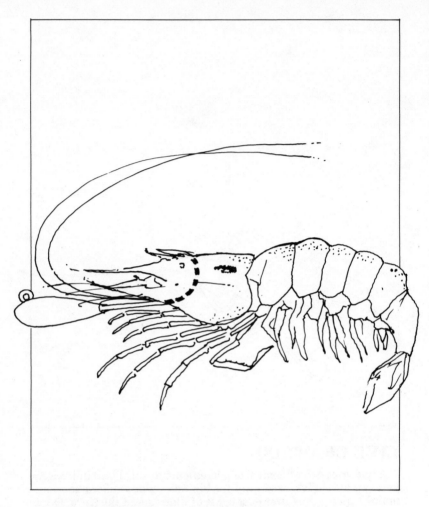

LIVE SHRIMP WITH JIG HEAD

Although many rigs incorporate artificial lures with dead, cut or rigged baits, not many combine live bait with artificials. The reason is obvious: artificial lures must be given motion by the angler in order to produce efficiently; live baits are generally left to provide their own movement, which should be as natural and unfettered as possible.

A certain few lure-live bait combinations, however, rank among the best of all fish-catchers. In salt water one of the leading examples is the marriage of a live shrimp and a leaded jig-head. One such head, the Trol-Rite is marketed for just that purpose, but any leaded hook—whether salvaged from an old jig or purchased new—will serve as well.

Since this rig does its best work right smack on bottom, the weight of the jig may have to be juggled in order to obtain the desired depth. In coastal shallows, one-quarter ounce is the usual size, but a half-ounce often is needed, and sometimes a head weighing up to an ounce is used in deeper channels and passes, particularly when there is strong current.

Start the point of the hook under the shrimp's "chin" and bring it out the top of the head—taking care to avoid damaging the dark spot which is visible in the head of the shrimp.

Make a long cast either directly upcurrent, or upcurrent and quartering away. Be sure to allow the rig to sink all the way to bottom, then retrieve just fast enough to keep a tight line as it works down with the current. You will, however, have to help keep it moving at times by very softly lifting the rodtip a few inches and increasing your retrieve rate just slightly. With a bit of practice you develop a "feel" for crawling the gadget along bottom, and your lifts of the rod at intervals impart a natural up-and-down movement to the shrimp.

The Trol-Rite also can be fished effectively where there is no current at all. In this case, simply make a long cast and, again, allow it to sink to bottom. Holding your rodtip right at the surface, turn your reel crank v-e-r-y slowly—more slowly, probably, than you have ever retrieved a lure in your life, even an artificial worm. Just a bit too much speed and the shrimp will go off keel and begin to turn. With a creeping pace, however, the shrimp will move upright and naturally, with its legs churning.

No need even to attempt listing the species of fish a jig-live shrimp combination attracts, since just about everything from large game fish to panfish (and, unfortunately, trash fish as well) love a slow-moving shrimp.

In certain situations, the combination of a jig head with a live baitfish can also be used with effect. One such instance would be for "hanging" a baitfish deep in a moving current where game fish are foraging. Hook the bait through both lips, let it out in the current, and when the desired position is reached, lock the reel and then either hold it or place it in a rod holder.

Hooked upward through the lips, the baitfish will hold a pretty normal attitude, facing into the current like a free-swimming fish, and the jig head helps hold it upright most of the time.

The bait will do a bit of swinging, and even turn on its side at times, but this is all to the good, since a sudden flash or a quick movement that simulates a fish in distress often touches off a strike.

Another application of the jig-baitfish rig is to cover a desired path of retrieve, as with the jig-shrimp. Cast the bait out and bring it back at a creeping pace over the selected course. Remember that a fast, or even a medium, retrieve rate will probably cause the baitfish to twist.

For bass fishing, a live shiner fished in the described manner will often outproduce a shiner that's simply left to wiggle in one spot.

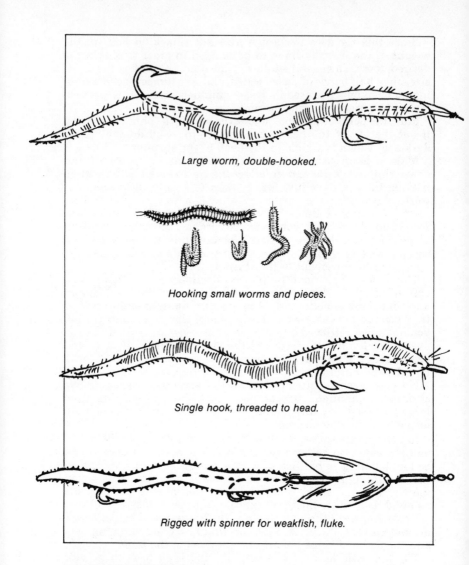

Large worm, double-hooked.

Hooking small worms and pieces.

Single hook, threaded to head.

Rigged with spinner for weakfish, fluke.

MARINE WORMS

Soft-bodied marine worms (sandworms, bloodworms, clam-worms, etc.) are excellent all-around baits and one of the most popular along the Middle and North Atlantic coasts. As shown in the small illustrations, chunks, pieces or whole tiny worms can be used for panfish—perhaps even several tiny worms on a single hook. Larger worms, rigged to a single or double hook, or behind a spinner, make excellent trolling, drifting or still-fishing baits for larger prey, such as weakfish, striped bass and flounder. An easy double hookup is accomplished with the Stinger Rig, shown in Chapter 3.

Rigged Baits

BALLYHOO (BALAO)

Once you learn it—and it doesn't take long—the ballyhoo is the simplest and fastest-to-rig of all offshore trolling baits. This, combined with the fact that it is an excellent producer of everything from marlin to mackerel, makes the ballyhoo top choice among both professional and private skippers.

The rigged ballyhoo is most often trolled at the surface, skipping across the waves. But it is rigged in exactly the same fashion for deep-trolling with a sinker; or for drift-fishing, either with a free line or with a sinker.

First step in making a ballyhoo rig is to leave a "pin" in your wire leader after wrapping on the hook. Study the illustration. The pin should be at right angles to the leader, and pointing in the opposite direction from the hook. The leader wrap, of course, is made with the Haywire twist as usual. Only difference is that you do not break off the excess wire; you cut off the excess, leaving enough for the pin.

Now take a piece of copper wire (which you buy in pre-cut lengths

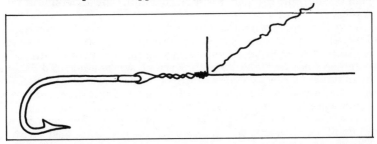

at the tackle store) and wrap one end of it several times around the leader wire at the base of the pin.

If ballyhoo is frozen, thaw it in a bucket of sea water before rigging.

Take the ballyhoo in your hands and bend it back and forth several times. This breaks the soft spine and makes the bait more flexible, so that it will have a more enticing swimming action and will be less likely to twist in the water.

* * *

Now you're ready to rig the ballyhoo to the hook.

Hold the ballyhoo in your left hand, and with your left thumb lift up the gill cover.

With your right hand, insert the hook point under the gills, into the body cavity. Work the point as far back as you can (bending the ballyhoo with your left hand helps here), and bring the point out on the underside of the bait.

When the point emerges, pull on it gently—just enough to bring the eye of the hook under the gill cover, and the leader pin under

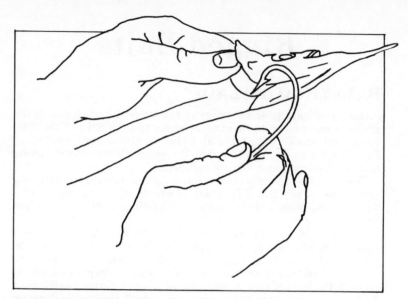

the "chin" of the ballyhoo, forward of the eyes.

Insert the pin upward, through both jaws of the bait, and with your thumb, hold the leader wire flush against the underside of the "chin."

Take the copper wire and wrap it tightly around the entire head TWICE behind the pin. Now wrap the copper wire around the head in front of the pin, and continue spiralling the wraps down the ballyhoo's bill for its full length. Keep all wraps snug, and finish by making your last couple of wraps very tight and close together near the end of the bill. Or, if you have a lot of excess copper wire, spiral some of it back up the bill toward the head again.

There is NO EXACT ROUTINE for wrapping the copper wire, so don't worry about whether you have each wrap "just right." The important points are simply to have the head wrapped tightly, so the pin will not slip out, and the bill wrapped snugly to the leader.

Your ballyhoo is now rigged and ready for trolling. It should skip the surface, or "swim" through the water without twisting. If it does twist, then an adjustment is necessary so crank the bait in.

Usually, a twisting bait means there is pressure on the hook. It

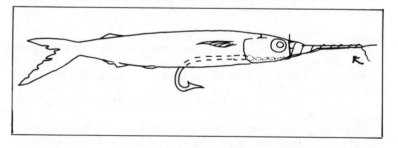

can be relieved by taking a knife point and enlarging the hole where the hook protrudes. Simply make a short slit with the knife point, thus extending the hole toward the head of the bait, in front of the hook.

NOTE ON HOOK SIZES: Ballyhoo come in various sizes, from about six inches long to more than a foot. Size of the average ballyhoo is around 10 inches. You may wish to buy both small and large ones for different purposes. Then, too, there are times you have to take what you can get, regardless of your preference. Because of this, you should keep at least three different hook sizes handy for your ballyhoo rigging.

For those tiny ballyhoo use a 5/0 or 6/0 hook; for average-size bait, a 7/0 or 8/0; for the largest ballyhoo, a 9/0 or 10/0.

ALTERNATE RIG: THE RUBBER BAND
(Not illustrated)

In rigging the ballyhoo, you may leave out the copper wire and use a tiny rubber band to hold the pin tightly in place. Drop the rubber band on the pin, stretch it around the head, and drop the other end over the pin. It may be necessary to stretch the rubber band twice around the head to assure a tight grip.

When using the rubber band instead of the copper wire, break the ballyhoo's bill off at the base.

Aside from substituting the rubber band for copper wire, this rig is made exactly the same way as previously described.

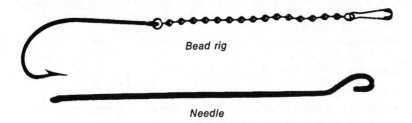

Bead rig

Needle

ALTERNATE RIG: THE BEAD CHAIN

The bead-chain rig comes ready-made and is purchased, complete with instructions, in your tackle store. Therefore, the rig is not illustrated here.

With the bead-chain, your hook is positioned near the tail of the bait, rather than forward. You insert the bait-needle in the ballyhoo's vent, and run the needle out the mouth. With the needle, you pull the bead-chain through, leaving the hook in position at the extreme rear of the abdominal cavity. Copper wire then is used to anchor the chain at the head, so there will be no pressure on the hook.

143

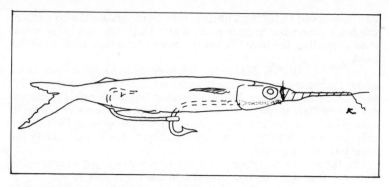

DOUBLE-HOOK BALLYHOO

A double-hook ballyhoo rig really isn't very satisfactory for trolling because the added hook seriously hampers the bait's action. Moreover, the second hook isn't necessary for most offshore fish and, in fact, can be a disadvantage in billfishing.

You may, however, use a double hook when drift-fishing—especially for kingfish, which have an uncanny knack for severing the ballyhoo just in back of the single hook.

The rig shown here is the easiest of all double-hook rigs, and is designed to thwart kingfish.

The second hook goes AFTER the bait is completely rigged; do not put it on before you rig, or you will be unable to rig in regular fashion at all.

Slip the eye of the second hook over the point of the first one, then press the point of the second hook upward into the bait. The flesh of a ballyhoo is soft, and the teeth of a kingfish sharp. He will get hooked even though the point of the hook is buried.

There are two main ways of attaching the second hook:

1. Pry open the eye of the second hook, then press the eye closed again with pliers after the hook is in place.

2. With pliers, bend down the barb of the first hook just enough to permit the eye of the second to slip over it. Then pry the barb back to its original position with the blade of a screwdriver.

FINGER MULLET, CIGAR MINNOW

This is the rig to use with finger mullet, cigar minnows or other small fish you may wish to troll.

Almost any type of small fish makes an acceptable trolling bait in an emergency, and if you get the chance to fish in foreign waters you might be faced with having to rig an unfamiliar species. Study the shape of the fish and the contour of its head, then decide whether to rig it in the fashion of the ballyhoo, or in the manner described here.

With this rig you do not use a "pin" of leader wire. In fact, you do not even attach your hook to the leader in advance.

Lay your hook alongside the bait, with the eye of the hook even with the eye of the fish. This is how you measure the approximate

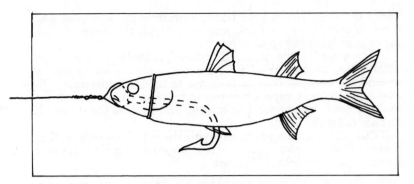

place where the hook point will come out of the fish's belly. Take the point of a knife and make a small slit in the belly at that spot.

Now insert the *eye* of the hook through that slit, into the belly, then forward through the throat and into the mouth.

Run the leader wire through the bottom jaw, through the eye of the hook, through the top jaw and out the top of the head. Pull enough wire through for ease of wrapping.

Last, wrap your leader wire close in front of the fish's lips, using the Haywire twist. Finish the wrap and break off excess.

As you can see, the pull will be on the loop of wire through the bait's head. There should be no pull on the hook. If the bait tends to twist, enlarge the hook hole with a knife point. It also helps to flex the bait back and forth to break the spine in one or more places.

LARGE MULLET

Large mullet are rigged in essentially the same way as finger mullet. However, the backbone must be removed, and there is some sewing involved.

You'll need a De-Boner (available in tackle stores) and a bait needle. Any kind of small braided line may be used as "sewing thread."

Large mullet are mainly employed in marlin and tuna fishing, but they take smaller species as well (to the distress of folks after big game). A large rigged mullet also makes a great bait for deep-trolling in quest of amberjack and heavy grouper.

TO PREPARE THE BAIT: Remove the entire backbone with the de-boner. If you haven't used one before, don't fret. It is much like coring an apple. The de-boner is a hollow tube with a sharp edge. Insert the edge under the gill, get it into position in front of the backbone, pointing toward the tail. With a slow, twisting motion, work the de-boner back for almost the full length of the fish. Bend the tail of the fish sideways and make a last gentle push with the de-boner to sever the spine. Remove the de-boner and the entire backbone comes with it. A rod (supplied with the de-boner when you buy it) is used to expel the backbone.

Now make a slit in the belly, large enough so that you can remove all the mullet's entrails. Insert the eye of your hook in this slit and push it forward into position inside the mullet's mouth, directly under the eyes. Insert your leader wire through both jaws and through the eye of the hook, exactly as with the finger mullet. Make your leader wrap as before.

It is now necessary to tie the gills closed, so that trolling pressure will not tear the bait. You CAN simply tie a piece of string tightly around the head, in back of the eyes, to hold the gills down. To avoid all chance of slippage, however, run your string through the mullet's head, using your bait needle, and then tie the string off tightly under the head.

If the belly slit you made in removing the entrails is so large that it seems likely to catch water and tear while trolling, then use your needle to sew the belly slit closed.

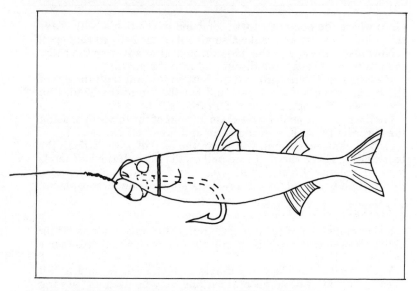

LEADED OR SWIMMING MULLET

To make the mullet remain under the surface and "swim," you incorporate an egg sinker into the rigging already described.

The leaded mullet is more or less standard for bluefin tuna fishing. Many marlin anglers and pot-luck offshore trollers like to troll both leaded and unleaded mullet baits at the same time. In rough seas, where skipping baits might be in the air as much as in the water, the lead helps keep the baits where they belong.

Obviously, finger mullet and cigar minnows can also be leaded if the angler desires, but with a smaller sinker, of course.

TO RIG THE LEAD: Slide your egg sinker onto the leader wire before inserting the wire through the head of the fish and the hook. After the wire is inserted through the bait and in position for wrapping, slide the sinker down and hold it under the bait's "chin" while you make as tight a wrap as possible.

Size of the egg sinker varies, but is usually one or two ounces.

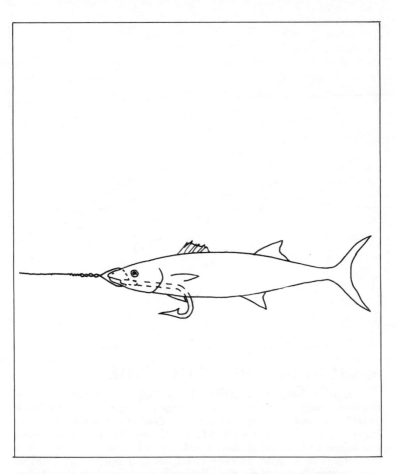

RIGGING MACKEREL, BARRACUDA

Mackerel, small barracuda, small bonefish and other species can be rigged with hook inside, exactly the same way as for mullet. All make good trolling baits for larger species of game fish, especially marlin.

With mackerel and small barracuda it usually is not necessary to de-bone, as you can make the bait limber enough simply by flexing it and breaking the spine in several places. De-boning is not so necessary for baits intended to skip the surface, as it is for baits intended to "swim."

Whether to de-bone or not, in a given situation and with a given bait, is largely your own decision.

In almost every case, however, it will be necessary to sew or tie the gills closed. With mackerel, you should also sew the belly cavity around the hook, even if your original hook-slit is not large. Mackerel flesh is very soft and tears easily.

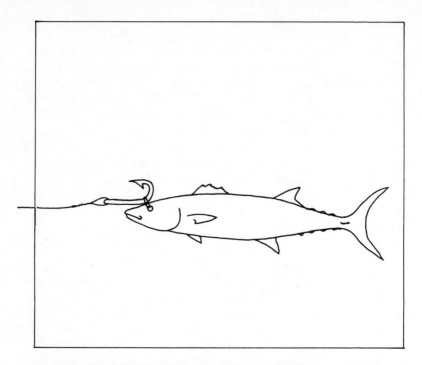

MARLIN RIG, HOOK OUTSIDE

In marlin fishing, the larger baits such as mackerel, bonito, bonefish, jack, dolphin, etc. are frequently rigged with the hook outside the bait. This rig is especially desirable when seeking the biggest possible marlin on 80 and 130-lb.-test line, and when using the biggest of gamefish hooks—12/0 to 15/0, or even 20/0. It is sometimes used with smaller baits, smaller hooks and light or medium tackle, but a rig with the hook inside is generally chosen for those applications.

With giant bait and an outside hook, the baitfish normally requires no preparation at all. You use it as is, with no de-boning or cutting—although the gills and mouth should be sewed tight.

TO RIG THE OUTSIDE HOOK: Take your bait needle, and thread a length of braided line through the eye sockets of the fish, remove the needle and tie the line tightly. Leave the ends of the sewing line long enough so they can be wrapped two or three times around the bend of your hook and tied again.

Some anglers rig in this same way, although running the tying line through both lips of the fish, instead of through the eye sockets. Most, however, prefer the eye tieup.

A BETTER METHOD THAN EITHER is to use a metal figure-eight as an attachment between the hook and the eye tieup. This method is explained under the instructions for Rigging Live Bonito. Refer to that section, as the rig is exactly the same whether the bait is alive or dead.

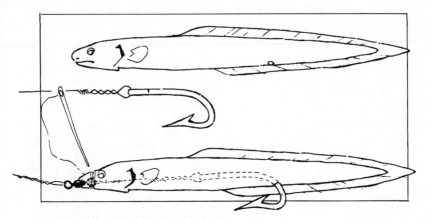

EEL FOR TROLLING

To rig an eel for trolling, first wrap your hook to the leader wire, using the Haywire Twist. Then place the bend of the hook at the eel's vent and measure the wire so you can wrap on a swivel at the mouth. Once the swivel is affixed to the other end of the short wire, insert a bait needle into the vent and use it to pull the swivel through the body cavity and into position in the mouth.

Sew the back eye of the swivel securely to the mouth, wrapping the thread tightly around the head as well. Make sure there is no pull at the hook: enlarge the opening slightly with a knife point if necessary. With a Haywire Twist, attach your leader to the front eye of the swivel.

In addition to being a great bait for offshore big-game fish, the rigged eel is excellent closer to shore for striped bass, blues and even big snook.

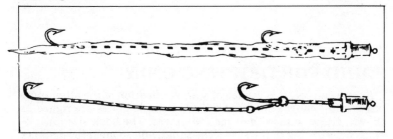

RIGGING AN EELSKIN

Here's the "plumber's special"—the main components being a length of brass chain and a rubber stopper with lip. The hooks can be affixed with split rings or double-ended snaps. The preserved eelskin is simply fitted over the chain and tied snugly behind the lip of the stopper, with hooks positioned one near the front and the other at the rear. A couple of small slits in the tough eelskin at the head permit water to enter and fill out the shriveled skin as you troll—making it quite fresh and lifelike in appearance.

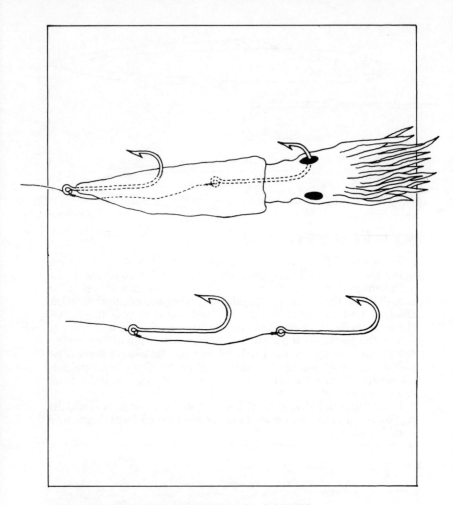

SQUID FOR DRIFTING ONLY

As you can see, this is basically an application of the all-purpose Stinger Rig shown in Chapter 3. Two single hooks are rigged as shown, either with wire or monofilament. The hook size must be gauged according to the size of the squid, and so must the distance between the hooks.

Insert the point of the front hook into the end of the tail, and out as shown. The rear hook is simply pushed through the head of the bait from the underside.

When drifting at night for swordfish, this rig is entirely adequate, and holds up well because there is no heavy pressure on the bait. Still, most professional skippers who swordfish by drifting at night do rig their baits as carefully as for trolling. Maybe its mostly for the sake of their image.

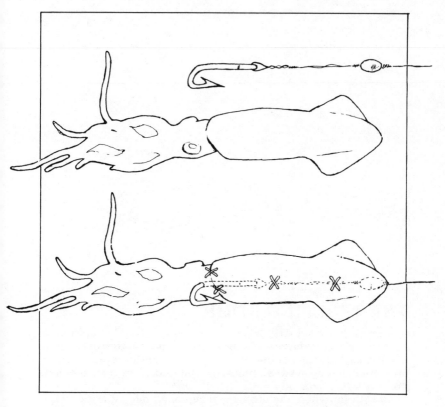

SQUID FOR TROLLING OR DRIFTING

Small rigged squids are one of the most popular baits for white marlin, and squids are effective as well for most species of billfish and tuna. Larger squids, of course, are used with bigger hooks for giants such as blue marlin and swordfish. Large squids, rigged in this fashion, are pretty much standard in the relatively new sport of night-drifting for swordfish, which originated in Florida but has now spread to many other coastal areas of the U.S. and abroad. Note, though, that drifting does not put nearly so much pressure on a bait as does trolling. The rig which follows is much faster and can be used instead of this one for drifting.

To rig the trolling squid, you must first measure with hook and leader so that you can tie or wrap in a small egg sinker at the point where it will snug up against the squid's "tail," with the hook in position in the head, just in front of its juncture with the mantle.

Insert a bait needle into the firm part of the head, between the eyes, and draw the leader inside the mantle its full length until the sinker comes into illustrated position. Sew the mantle to the leader, and reinforce the connection of head to mantle at the places marked, with X-shaped stitches.

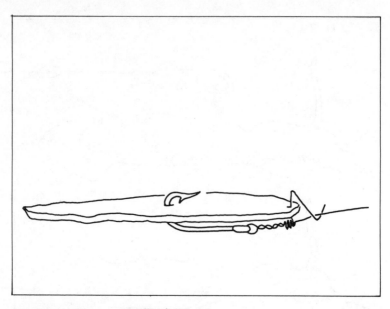

THE TROLLING STRIP

A properly-rigged strip is one of the best trolling baits. Private anglers seldom make use of it because it is more bother to rig than a ballyhoo, but many of the more successful charter captains insist on keeping a strip out at all times (in combination with other baits), and the strip frequently outfishes the rest.

As with ballyhoo, the strip rig requires a "pin" of leader wire. But note that in this case the pin points in the same direction as the hook, and you leave a much longer pin than for ballyhoo.

The most desirable strips are those cut from the white underparts of a bonito. Belly sections of mackerel, kings, dolphin, barracuda and other fish can be used. Mullet strips work well but are less durable.

The strip should be about 10 or 12 inches long and trimmed to teardrop shape—with a short taper at the hook end; a longer taper at the rear. Carefully trim off excess flesh so that the strip is no more than a quarter-inch thick, preferably less than that. The thinner the strip, the more action. But a thin layer of flesh must be maintained so the bait will hold shape.

TO RIG THE STRIP: Insert the pin through the strip at the short-tapered front end. Study the illustrations and note that the pin must now be bent forward and secured on the leader, ahead of the bait. To do this, take pliers and bend a tiny V-shaped or U-shaped catch at the end of the pin, so that it can be fixed to the leader in much the same manner as a safety pin.

Now the strip must be bunched forward slightly while you insert the hook. After the hook is in place, the strip must lie perfectly flat. There must be no pressure from the hook on the strip. If there is, enlarge the hook hole with a knife point to relieve the pressure.

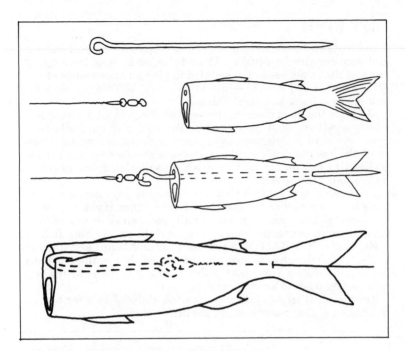

GULF COAST TARPON RIG

This is the standard bait for tarpon fishing over much of the Gulf Coast. It is fished directly on bottom, lying there until picked up by a tarpon (or a shark if you're unlucky). When a tarpon takes this bait, allow him to travel with it as you keep your reel in free-spool. After a few seconds, when you think he has swallowed the bait deep, tighten your line gently, then strike hard.

The rig should not be used unless your plan is to kill and keep the tarpon, for most tarpon caught this way will not live if released.

CAUTION: Sometimes the tarpon feels the hook and will start to jump before you've planned to strike. If you observe the beginning of a jump, tighten your line fast and strike immediately.

For this rig, make up your leader in advance. Use a six-foot leader of 100 or 120-pound-test monofilament; or a six-foot leader of 90 or 135-pound-test wire cable.

If monofilament is used, tie a stout swivel to one end of the leader, a 10/0 hook to the other. The ties can be made with either the Improved Clinch Knot or the Two-Wrap Hangman's Knot. In either case, use pliers and a lot of pressure to make sure the knots are drawn down tight.

If cable is used, attach the hook and swivel with sleeve and crimper.

TO RIG: Cut the head off a mullet. Run a bait needle the full length of the mullet, alongside the backbone, coming out at the tail. Hook the eye of the needle to your swivel and pull your complete leader through the bait, so the hook is positioned as shown.

CUT FISH

Cut baits and unrigged whole dead baits are used for still-fishing, and occasionally for drifting. They differ, as a class, from rigged baits in that they are not calculated to give an appearance of live action. Nor is any special rigging necessary. You simply stick the bait on your hook and start fishing.

Mullet is the most commonly used fish for cut bait, because it is widely available and inexpensive. You can also cut baits from most any kind of fish you might catch with the cut mullet. Naturally, the fish you don't want to take home are the ones you're most inclined to cut up for bait—pinfish or sailor's choice, ladyfish, jack, small grunts, etc.

However, if you get in a tight spot for bait, don't hesitate to cut baits from one of your "eating" fish. For instance, if you're drifting for speckled trout and run out of bait, you can fillet one of your smaller trout, cut strips from it, and go right on catching fish.

HOW TO CUT BAIT: Always use a cutting board and a sharp knife. The fish may or may not be scaled, but scaling usually helps. Slice fillets from both sides of the fish; discard the rest (unless you wish to use the head for bait).

From each fillet you can cut squarish slabs of bait for bottom fishing, or rather narrow strips for drift fishing.

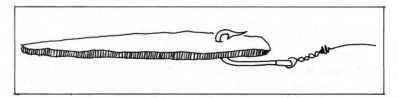

STRIP FOR DRIFTING

If drift-fishing (speckled trout, etc.) take a rough-cut strip and hook it through one end, as shown in the illustration. There is no need to rig the strip, or taper it, as you would for trolling.

STRIP OR CHUNK FOR BOTTOM FISHING

If bottom-fishing, use either a rough strip or a chunk and run your hook through the bait twice (three or more times if using a bait large enough to permit it).

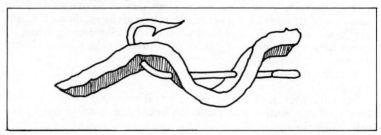

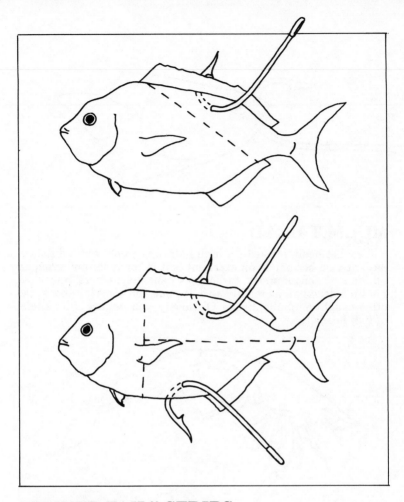

"SHINER TAIL" STRIPS

Good baits for either trolling or bottom fishing can be cut from small fish such as pinfish. These are called "shiner tails" and widely used in trout-fishing. But these baits produce a variety of fish in many waters.

One illustration shows a single bait, cut diagonally from the tail. The other shows how you can cut the entire tail half from the pinfish, then cut it again lengthwise to make two baits. With either method, you cut all the way through the fish (that is, you don't just slice off one fillet), and use the bait with bone in.

Such a bait is more durable than a strip of fillet, since it withstands the nibbles of "bait stealers" while waiting for a good strike.

The head sections make good bottom bait for snapper, grouper or big redfish. The prepared "tails" are good for either drifting or bottom fishing.

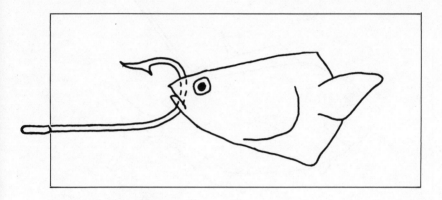

MULLET HEAD

A mullet head, hooked through both lips as shown and fished patiently on bottom, is an excellent bait for snapper and grouper on the reefs, or for snook, tarpon, jewfish, etc., inshore. Snook do not hit a dead bait as readily as a live one, but some big snook are often caught on mullet heads. Obviously, you can use other kinds of fish heads too.

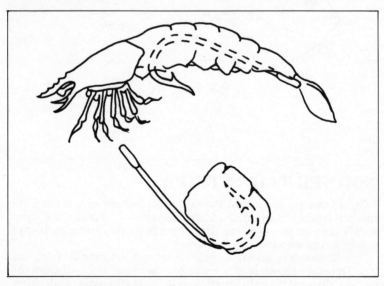

DEAD SHRIMP

Dead shrimp may be used whole, broken in half, or cut in small pieces.

If used whole, thread the shrimp on the hook as shown. Half a shrimp should be threaded in much the same way.

For panfish, use tiny pieces of shrimp, with the skin peeled off, and cover the point of the hook as illustrated.

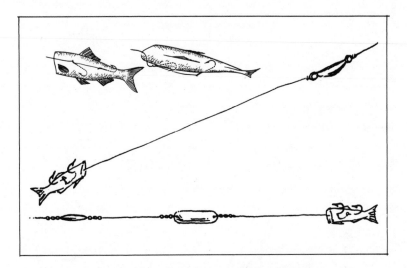

CUT PLUG BAIT FOR MOOCHING

To rig a herring or similar baitfish for "mooching" in the traditional style of salmon fishermen in the Northwest, first cut off the head, slanting the cut slightly rearward. Remove entrails. Now use our old friend, the Stinger Rig, shown in Chapter 3. Again, hook size must be appropriate to the size of the bait. Insert the front hook in at the head and out the side. The rear hook goes in and out either the side of the fish or the dorsal surface.

The mooching bait is drifted out and is worked by the current in an erratic, wobbling and spinning motion. Or it may be slow trolled. In either case it can be rigged to a weightless leader when conditions permit, but more often is used in combination with a trolling sinker to obtain the desired depth, as in the second illustration. The third drawing shows how a flasher or dodger can be incorporated into the leader ahead of the plug bait for additional attractiveness.

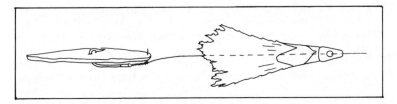

FEATHER AND STRIP

An extremely popular combination for trolling offshore or on the reef is the feather-strip.

The trolling feather is threaded to your leader, after which you rig a strip for trolling as described earlier. In use, the feather slides down to the hook, covering the forward portion of the strip.

157

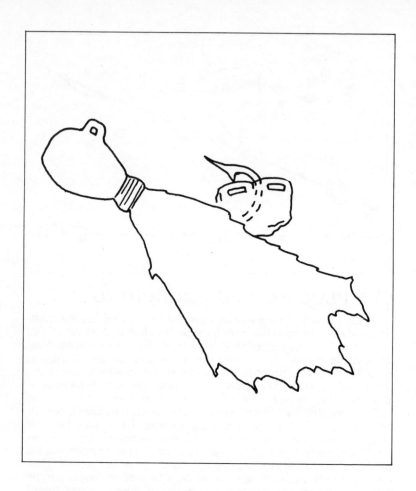

JIG WITH SHRIMP

When you add a small "tip" of cut shrimp to an artificial jig you come up with the one best casting lure of all for the Gulf Coast. The same combo clicks for bonefish, and much Atlantic Coast fishing as well.

You will catch many more redfish and trout with a tipped jig than with a bare jig. You will also catch bottom-feeders, such as sheepshead and drum, which rarely if ever hit a plain jig. At the same time, the tip of shrimp does not hinder the action of the bait and so you catch just as many snook and tarpon—maybe more, although this is a point of debate among anglers.

But to make the jig work right, you have to use a *small* piece of shrimp. Too large a piece causes the jig to twist on the retrieve.

You get more tips from a single shrimp if you cut them with a knife, rather than breaking them off with your fingers.

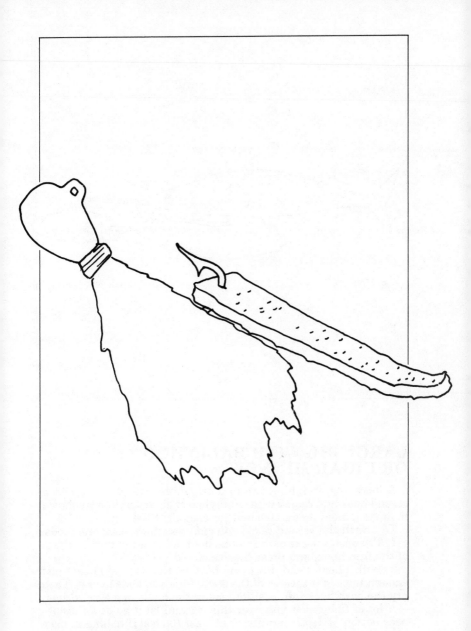

JIG WITH STRIP

A small strip of cut fish or squid can be used in place of the shrimp. It does not work so well as the shrimp for a wide range of Gulf Coast fish, but often pays off handsomely when you're fishing for mackerel or bluefish.

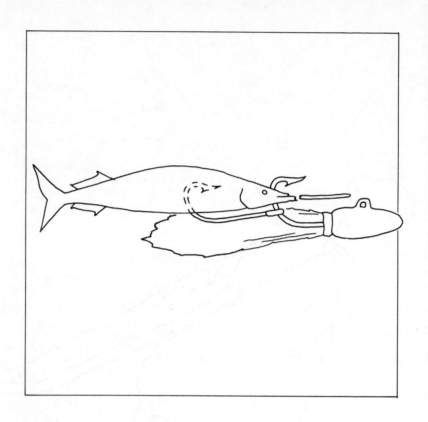

LARGE JIG WITH BALLYHOO
OR CIGAR MINNOW

A heavy jig, weighing two to four ounces, can be fitted with a second hook and rigged with a ballyhoo or cigar minnow as shown to make a most productive bait for deep drift fishing.

To attach the second hook, you can use either of two methods:

1. Pry open the eye of the second hook, slip it over the barb of the first hook, and press the eye closed.

2. With pliers, bend down the barb of the hook slightly—just enough to permit the eye of the second hook to slide over it. Then pry the barb back into position, using the blade of a screwdriver.

A lot of fishermen toss over this rig and let it go down deep—near bottom if depth permits, or at least 100 feet if fishing in deep blue water. They use the rig on a stout boat rod, and place the rod in a holder with the reel in gear, but the drag set fairly light. Most any fish which takes will hook itself. This rig has taken a great many big grouper, snapper, kingfish and even quite a few sailfish.

If kingfish are hitting, you may wish to add a third hook, since kings are notorious short-strikers. Rig the third hook exactly as you did the second.

160

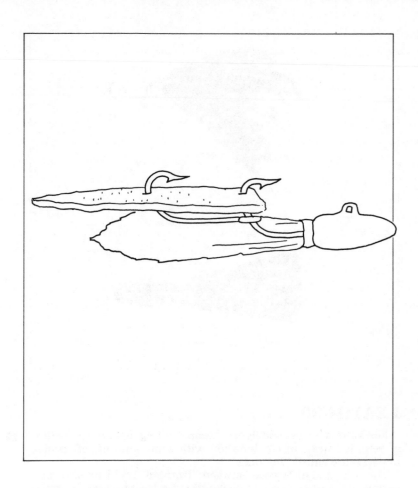

LARGE JIG WITH STRIP

A deep jig with a strip can be used in precisely the same way as described for the ballyhoo—on a drifting line down deep.

But it is more frequently used as a king mackerel rig when kings are schooling, and is one of the best. Use a nylon jig, weighing one or one-and-a-half ounces. Attach a second hook (see above for methods), and hook on the strip as shown.

Cast it out, let it sink to or beyond the suspected level of the kingfish, then retrieve it with sweeps of the rod. Kings will hit it while it sinks, or during the retrieve.

There is also a good rig for bottom-jigging. Let it sink all the way to bottom, then bounce it around a few times without retrieving any line. If a grouper or snapper is around, chances are he'll hit. If no strike occurs at bottom, retrieve all the way to the boat with sharp upward sweeps of the rod, cranking in line between sweeps. You can catch kings or other mid-depth species on the way in.

FEATHERS

For want of a more widely-used term, trolling lures which feature a weighted head in combination with some kind of soft trailer material are called "feathers."

The principal difference between "feathers" and lead-head jigs is that the feathers are supplied without a built-in hook, whereas jigs have the hook molded into the head.

Often the trailer material is really of feathers, and at one time all such lures were made with feathers—hence the popular name which has hung on. Nowadays, nylon is commonly used as trailer material. You also see this type of lure made sometimes with plastic streamers and, rarely, with hair.

Feathers come in a wide assortment of sizes, and are used mostly for offshore trolling. You run your leader wire through the hollow head, and attach the hook of your choice.

The feather is often rigged in combination with a strip of bait, as described previously.

Any ocean gamefish will at times hit the plain trolled feather, and for a lot of offshore species, the feather alone seems just about as productive as the feather-strip combination.

Most popular colors are solid yellow, solid white, or mixtures of either color with red.

162

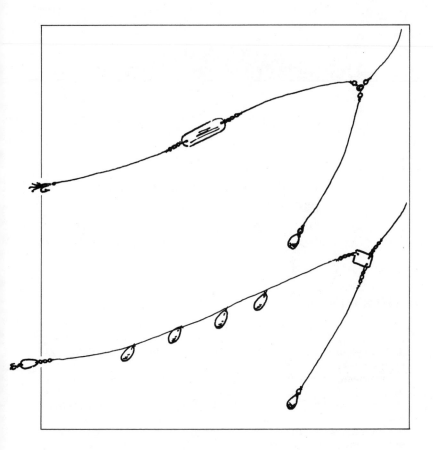

DODGERS, FLASHERS, BELLS

A variety of shiny ornaments strung ahead of the trolled lure have proven effective for many different kinds of gamefish, and in far-flung areas. Though most-used in deep trolling for trout and salmon—on the Pacific Coast, in the Great Lakes and other deep lakes—these elaborate getups also have proved their mettle in salt-water for bluefish and other species.

As illustrated, the large metal flashers and dodgers are built into the leader by means of swivels at each end of the device. The strings of spinners or wobblers generally are purchased ready-made, although a few anglers do rig up their own.

The illustrations show a spoon and a streamer fly as the trailing lures, but many other lures can be used too. Let preferences of the various fishing areas guide you on this.

To get the rig deep, a bank or dipsey swivel is used on a dropper line, as shown.

SPOONS

Perhaps the most versatile of all saltwater trolling lures is the silver spoon. Many models, in many sizes, are made by a number of different manufacturers. Most popular *trolling* spoons have fixed single hooks.

Size designation for saltwater trolling spoons are by number. Most-used sizes are between No. 1 (small) and No. 7 (large). Bigger spoons than No. 7 may be used for giant tarpon, or for offshore species.

Unfortunately, those numbers denote relative size only in spoons of the same brand. One company's No. 2 may be another company's No. 5.

Another way to gauge spoon size is by hook size. Most spoons do name the hook size on their packaging.

Here is a short table which may help you select a spoon of appropriate size:

Type Fishing	Hook Size
Inshore trolling (mackerel, blues, etc.)	1/0 - 3/0
Inshore trolling (snook, reds, small tarpon)	3/0 - 6/0
Offshore trolling (kingfish, etc.)	6/0 and up
Big tarpon trolling	6/0 - 9/0

This table is a general guideline. Variations are common among different anglers.

Some spoons come with a built-on swivel. You should *always* use a swivel ahead of a spoon to prevent line twist, so if your spoon has no swivel, be sure to use one between leader and line.

See the Wire-Wrapping section of this book for a special rig that provides extra action when trolling a spoon.

See more about spoons in section on Artificial Lures.

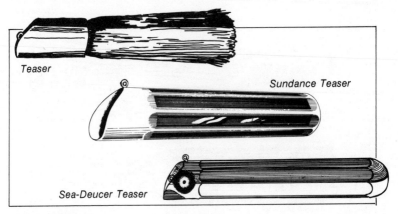

Teaser

Sundance Teaser

Sea-Deucer Teaser

TEASERS

Teasers are oversized lures without hooks, used to make a commotion while trolling and thus entice marlin, sails and other sought-after game fish to the vicinity of your trolled baits.

Almost every experienced skipper likes to use a teaser while billfishing.

Manufacturered teasers may simply be huge wooden plugs, or wooden plugs with trailing skirts of nylon. Empty bottles or empty cans with holes punched in both ends are often used as teasers.

The teaser is rigged to a heavy wire leader, which in turn is tied, by means of a big swivel, to a stout rope or cord. The cord is snubbed around a cleat on the transom of the boat. Most teasers are trolled only 20 feet or so behind the boat.

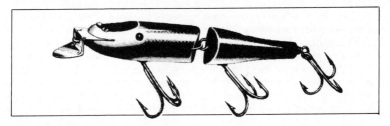

TROLLING PLUGS

Any diving or sinking plug can be trolled as well as cast. Almost all plugs trolled inshore are simply casting plugs in popular models, such as the Darter, Sea Bee, Rebel, Mirrolure, Bomber, Pikie and numerous others.

A few *very large* plugs are manufacturered specifically for saltwater trolling—mainly for tarpon but also for offshore species.

Though not used nearly as often as they should be by veteran offshore anglers, big plugs with extra-strength hooks produce a lot of strikes from kingfish. And plugs which run deep are surprisingly effective over the reefs for grouper and snapper.

See section on artificial lures.

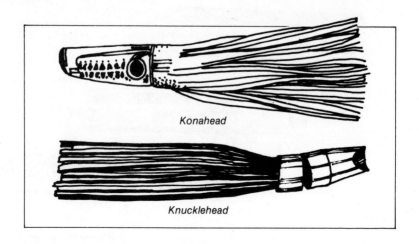

Konahead

Knucklehead

BLUEWATER TROLLING LURES

Big-game fishermen in all waters of the world are turning more and more to artificial lures for deepsea trolling. Long used in Hawaii and other waters of the Pacific, lures are now well established, too, on most marlin grounds of the South Atlantic, Gulf of Mexico and Caribbean.

Typically, the big marlin lures feature a hard plastic head and a plastic skirt. There are several basic head designs, each providing a different action and each generally requiring a different range of trolling speeds to bring out its best performance. Tapered or torpedo heads offer the least water resistance. They are straight runners and can be trolled at the fastest speeds. Flathead lures are currently the most popular style in most big-game areas. They also run straight, but their blunt heads kick up more commotion. Flatheads can be used at high speeds—up to 20 knots—although most anglers prefer to drag them at about 9 or 10 knots. Lures with a slanted, concave head, such as the long-familiar Konaheads, have an erratic, darting action, and for this reason are often used as teasers as well as actual lures. Because they aren't straight runners, they are usually pulled at the low end of the lure-speed range, eight knots or so, although somewhat faster speeds may be used.

Artificial lures eliminate the "drop-back," which is standard procedure in attempting to hook a billfish which strikes a natural rigged bait. Marlin will often track an artificial, but just as often, the strike comes suddenly and savagely, and the fish is either on or off before the angler has much chance to influence the result.

These lures may be trolled directly off the rod, with the reel in strike-drag position. But most veteran anglers and captains much prefer to provide an elastic resistance to a striking fish. This they do by running a "stinger" line off the outrigger line. At the end of the stinger line is a heavy-duty snap. A rubber band is half-hitched to the fishing line and then the other end of the band is placed in

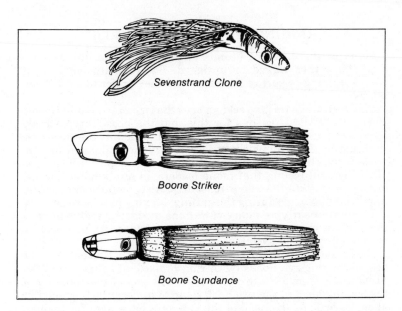

Sevenstrand Clone

Boone Striker

Boone Sundance

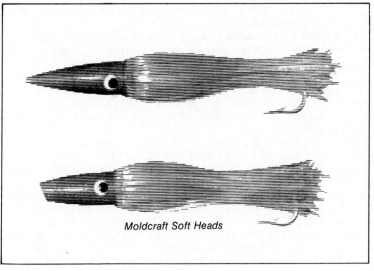

Moldcraft Soft Heads

the snap on the stinger line. When a marlin hits, both the "give" of the outrigger lines and the rubber band provide shock-absorption and yet there is enough pressure to set the hook before the line cuts through the rubber band and breaks it.

After the fishing line comes tight to the fish, additional hook-setting tactics of a traditional nature can be employed—gunning the engines briefly and striking with the rod.

167

RIGGING THE TROLLING LURES

Many of the different brands of offshore or marlin lures are available either rigged or unrigged. For real afficionados, of course, rigging is part of the game and they prefer to do it themselves.

Single-strand wire is so seldom used that it can be shunted aside. There are several reasons for this, but the possibility of kink-breakage, particularly with erratic lures, is probably the main one. With big artificial lures either very heavy monofilament or wire cable is the choice. Monofilament wins out in popularity because of the general feeling that mono leaders, in any kind of fishing, draw more strikes than do wire leaders. Also, mono is more easily handled at boatside during the gaffing, tagging or release process.

There are nearly as many variations in rigging preferences as there are in lures. If you haven't developed your own preferences, try the following procedure:

Hooks should be of forged, big-game patterns. In the rig to be described, ring-eye hooks (with ring braised, of course) are best. Sizes range from 10/0 to about 14/0. The gap of the hook—or of the leading hook in the two-hook setup to be described—should be about as wide as the head of the lure, or a bit wider. The trailing hook can be exactly the same, although many anglers prefer it to be one or two sizes smaller.

In addition to the hooks, you will need 300-pound monofilament for leader, 600-pound aircraft cable for joining the two hooks, a crimping tool and No. 11 sleeves.

Cut a piece of the monofilament to your chosen leader length. IGFA rules allow 30 feet in line classes heavier than 20 (with a 10-foot double line). To avoid later measurement problems caused by stretch and/or careless measuring to begin with, make the leader about 25 feet long.

"Ball" one end of the mono leader by holding a flame to it and pressing the heated end against a metallic object. Then form a simple loop at this same end and crimp as shown on page 81. Some anglers use a single sleeve, others two. If carefully crimped, a single should suffice. The other end of the leader is left alone for the present. It will later be threaded through the lure and crimped to the pre-rigged double hooks. And now to rigging the hooks:

Cut a piece of aircraft cable six or eight inches long. Run one end through the eye of the forward hook and crimp it. The other end is crimped to the eye of the trailing hook. A single loop and single sleeve is used in both these crimps, as in the first drawing on page 81. To conform to IGFA rules, the eyes of the two hooks must be at least a hook's length apart, and the trailing hook cannot extend more than a hook's length beyond the skirt of the lure.

Last, use electrician's tape to tape the cable tightly to the shank of the leading hook. Again, preferences as to the relative planes of the two hook-points vary, but most often the taping is done in such a way as to position the point of the trailing hook at right angles to the front one.

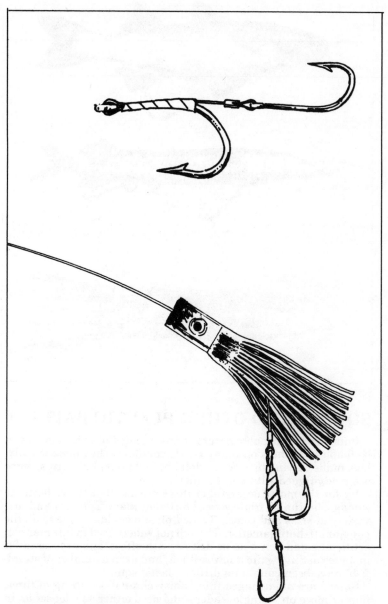

With several leaders prepared in advance, along with several of these two-hook sets, you can choose or change lures easily—having only to run the mono leader through the lure and crimp on the hooks. In attaching the leader to the hooks many anglers choose the type of loop shown on page 82, although others stick to the single loop.

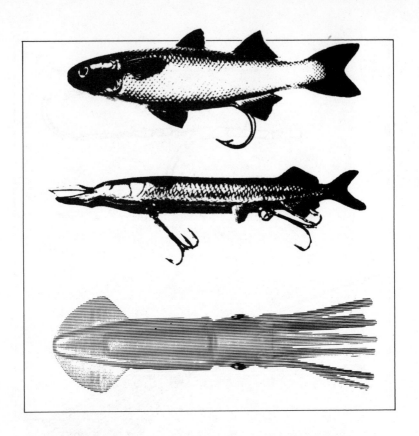

SQUIDS AND OTHER PLASTIC BAITS

Imitations of popular natural baits, molded of soft plastic, can be found nowadays on many tackle counters. They include bally-hoo, mullet, flying fish, squid, dolphin and even plain strips. Some are ready-rigged with short leaders.

By far the most successful of these molded baits have been the squids, obtainable from several different manufacturers and in a variety of sizes and colors. Trolled plastic squids will take all the popular offshore gamefish. Though not widely used in this manner, artificial squid can also be drifted with effect, and even used for inshore casting. Quite a few sailfish, and even a number of sword-fish, have been caught on drifted plastic squids.

Squids are often rigged into "daisy chains"—a string of three, four or more on a single leader—and used either as a teaser or, in some cases, as an actual trolling lure.

Rigging a daisy chain is easy. Just thread the desired number of squids onto a wire or heavy monofilament leader, then space them the desired distance apart—generally a foot or two—by fixing small Rubber-Cor sinkers at the selected spacing locations. A hook at the end of the leader completes the rig. No hook is added, of course, if the chain is to serve simply as a teaser.

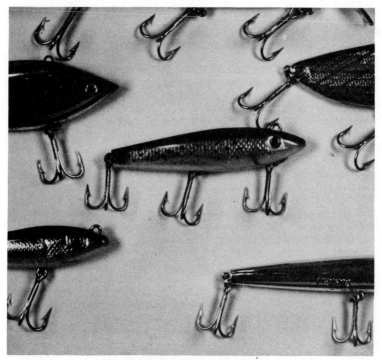

Artificial Lures

The term "artificial lure" or simply "artificial," refers to any device made of synthetic material that is intended to fool a fish into thinking it is natural food.

All artificials require some sort of motion to make them work. Usually the motion is provided either by casting the lure and retrieving it, or by trolling. Some lures work well with no more motion than merely allowing them to sink or settle slowly in the water. Others must be moved fast to draw strikes.

This section will cover artificial lures for both fresh and saltwater fishing. Many artificial lures are used both in salt and fresh water. With most of the others, the only difference between fresh and saltwater versions are in size and perhaps hook strength.

Certain artificial lures designed strictly for saltwater trolling have been covered already in the section on Saltwater Baits and Lures.

Obviously, there are far too many different lures to permit a comprehensive survey. Instead, this section will look at the major types of lures and discuss some of their uses.

The mention of brand names is necessary for easy identification of the types under discussion. However, such mention is for reference purposes only, and does not necessarily mean the named lures are better than others of their type.

SURFACE AND
FLOATING-DIVING PLUGS

Surface lures are the pets of many bass fishermen, and a lot of saltwater anglers. They are designed to splash the top of the water and imitate a distressed fish. Some surface plugs make more noise than others, according to design. And some surface plugs float while at rest, but dive under and "swim" on a straight retrieve. These are called floating-diving plugs and can be used either as a surface lure or underwater lure.

THE SLIM-MINNOW TYPES: These are slender, buoyant plugs, with small plastic lips. Some are made of balsa wood (Rapala, Bang-O-Lure), and some are made of plastic (Rebel, Sea Bee).

The balsa wood models have a bit more action, and are preferred by many freshwater fishermen. Plastic ones are tougher and better-suited for use in the sea. However, the plastic ones do work very well in fresh water, and many inland anglers prefer them if for no other reason than that they are much easier to cast.

Several good retrieves are possible with this type plug. Try twitching them on the surface two or three times with pauses in between. Also try retrieving them very slowly, so that they "swim" but stay atop the water. You can also impart a fast, darting retrieve to them by sweeping your rod as you wind in. Or you can simply wind at medium to fast speed and treat them as swimming, underwater lures.

As a surface lure, these are the best of all for use when the water is very calm. A noisier surface plug might scare more fish than it attracts.

THE DARTING TYPES: These are wooden or plastic plugs, designed so they will dig slightly into the water and dart when the rod is jerked. Examples are the Creek Chub Darter, Boone Spinana, etc. Darters have for many years been a standby lure of both bass fishermen, and snook fishermen. They also work well on tarpon and many other fresh and saltwater fish.

In fresh water, these plugs normally are allowed to lie still for up to a minute, then twitched two or three times with pauses in between. On the retrieve, they dive under and swim well, and many strikes come during this stage.

The standard saltwater action is much the same, except that little, if any, pause is allowed between jerks of the rod. This is an especially good lure for mangrove snook. The initial noise of the darting seems to draw them from under the roots. They might hit while the plug is being worked at the surface, but just as often they strike during the final retrieve—possibly because they think the distressed fish has recovered and is escaping.

THE POPPING TYPES: True popping plugs have hollowed or cup-faced heads (Example: Chugger, Plunker, Hula Popper). They make a loud "blurping" noise when jerked hard with the rod, but the angler can control the amount of noise by how softly or sharply he twitches his rod to cause the pop.

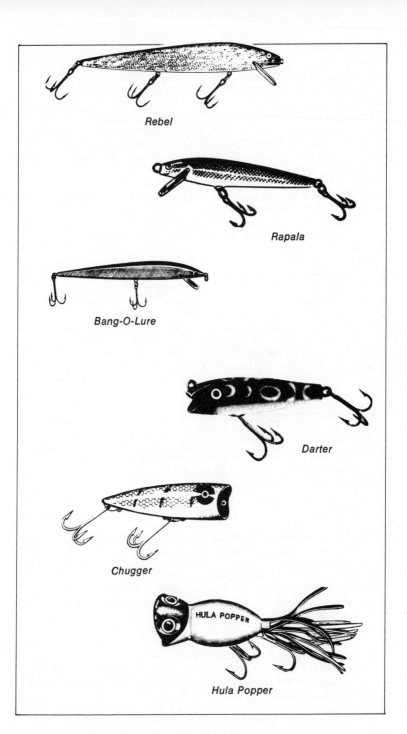

Rebel

Rapala

Bang-O-Lure

Darter

Chugger

HULA POPPER

Hula Popper

In fresh water, a rather soft pop is preferred, with a long pause before the next one. Sometimes, however, a loud pop pays off better —especially if there is considerable chop on the water.

The pop-and-pause retrieve is good, too, for shallow-water fishing along the coast.

Large popping plugs are one of the very best, and most exciting, of lures for casting in deeper salt waters—such as the reefs, or even the Gulf Stream at times. Special large poppers are used here, with heavy hooks that are wired through for strength. (Examples: Scudder, Chuggit.)

For offshore fishing, you have to use a stout rod, and then pop the lure as hard as you can and as fast as you can. The more fuss the better. A big popper on the reefs can take just about anything, including barracuda, jack, amberjack, tuna, mackerel, kingfish, bonito, sailfish—and even big bottom fish such as grouper and snapper.

CRIPPLED MINNOW TYPES: These are somewhat similar to the darters, except they are not designed to run under the surface at all. They are fitted with spinners, either at the tail or at both head and tail. (Examples: Dalton Special, Injured Minnow, Devil's Horse, Nip-I-Didee, Diamond Rattler.)

Though spinner-rigged plugs work in salt water, they have never become very popular. Most bass fishermen, however, keep some injured minnow plugs in their kits and use them avidly.

As with most freshwater surface plugs, this type works best with slow twitches and long pauses. Sometimes, especially at night, strikes come faster on a straight, slow retrieve with the propellers whirring steadily at the surface.

DANCING TYPES: These are torpedo shaped plugs, weighted slightly at the tail so they sit on the surface at an angle. (Examples: Zara Spook, Ballerina.) Much more popular in salt water than fresh, they can be made to dance along the surface by a fast retrieve and skillful manipulation of the rod tip. They are deadly for snook, jack and trout in particular.

Other good retrieves are possible, too. With a steady wind and a slow, rhythmic waving of the rod tip, they swim on the surface much like a mullet.

When the pop-and-pause technique is used with these plugs, they dive, then jump high out of the water while remaining in almost the same spot. For this reason, a lot of bass fishermen do like them very much and use them regularly.

FLOATING-DIVING: The slim minnow already has been mentioned as a floater-diver. But there is another type which has been popular in fresh water for many years. The two leading examples are the Lucky 13 and Bass Oreno. They can be made to pop almost as loudly as a true popping plug, but dive well under the surface and wiggle enticingly on a fast retrieve.

CRAWLING PLUGS: Chief example of this type is the Jitterbug. Crawlers are almost always worked with a straight, slow retrieve. They wobble or crawl across the surface with continuous noise, and are much chosen for night fishing because bass, it seems, can zero in on them much better than on a lure which alternates noise and silence.

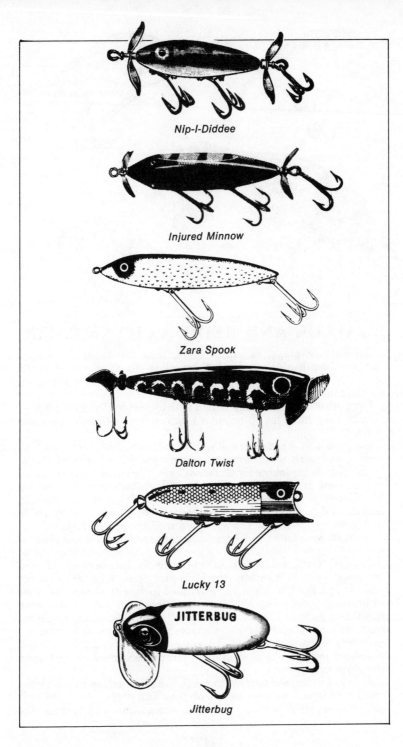

Nip-I-Diddee

Injured Minnow

Zara Spook

Dalton Twist

Lucky 13

Jitterbug

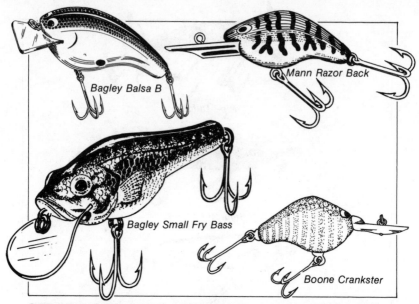

Bagley Balsa B

Mann Razor Back

Bagley Small Fry Bass

Boone Crankster

SHALLOW AND MEDIUM CRANK BAITS

Sub-surface plugs, or crank baits, that run from shallow to medium depth do not lend themselves to type-classification so easily as do surface lures. So labels will not be used except in obvious instances.

Let's start with the plugs which sink by virtue of weight alone—that is, they have no lip or other planing device to help get them down.

Some of these plugs are slow-sinkers, the most famous of all perhaps—in salt water anyway—being the 52 M series of Mirrolures. This is undoubtedly the most versatile saltwater plug of all for shallow fishing, and takes anything from trout to tarpon. Mirrolures of other series numbers are similar, but may vary in length, and in sinking rate. They may either be retrieved in rhythmic jerks, or else made to swim on a medium-speed retrieve.

In fresh water, one widely popular family of underwater plugs is the "shad-type." These have the general appearance of small shad minnows—flattened and thin, but relatively deep-bodied. Some of the many examples include the Thin Fin, Spot, Speed Shad, Sonic and Bayou Boogie. Most have molded-in lips that provide their swimming action. Others get their action from a deep, flattened head or a molded top fin. Anyway, all are shallow-running lures that take bass and a great variety of freshwater fish, and are excellent open-water lures. In some of the brands mentioned, weighted models are also offered, which run much deeper than the standard models.

Another prominent group, in much the same action category but vastly different appearance, are the "fat plugs" or "alphabet plugs"—so-called because they are, indeed, fat, and because the

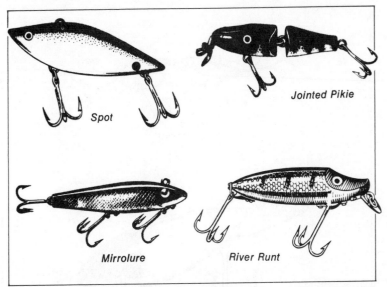

Spot

Jointed Pikie

Mirrolure

River Runt

original models were named by single letters—such as "Big O" and "Big B." These are lipped plugs which generally float at rest, but which are not commonly employed as surface poppers, although they can produce fish as such. As a class they are shallow runners but, again, some models have larger lips for deeper diving.

This type plug is effective on a straight retrieve, although you should vary the speed to test for best results. There is nothing in particular to be gained by "jigging" your rod as you retrieve these lures; however, it often pays to impart a variable retrieve simply by cranking-and-stopping, cranking-and-stopping.

Let's move now to another group of shallow-to-medium plugs— those with rather short metal lips. Some famous examples are the River Runt, Pikie, L&S lures, Cisco Kids. Their action is about the same as the shad types and others with molded lips. Some of them, particularly the Pikies, are old favorites in salt water as well as fresh, but usually in beefed-up models. They run a bit deeper on the average, than do the molded-lip plugs. Again, the best retrieve is a steady one with varying speeds.

Shallow-running plugs are excellent for trolling, as well as casting, whenever it isn't necessary to go down very deep. This holds for both salt and fresh water.

By trying different motor speeds to determine what pace brings out the best action, the unlipped Mirrolures are also great trolling baits for salt water.

Incidentally, many slow-sinking plugs can be fished effectively at great depth if you just take the time to let them sink before you retrieve. Try the "count down" method: Count slowly as your plug sinks, and note the count on which it hits bottom. Next cast, shorten the count by one or two numbers, and you should be skimming close to the bottom.

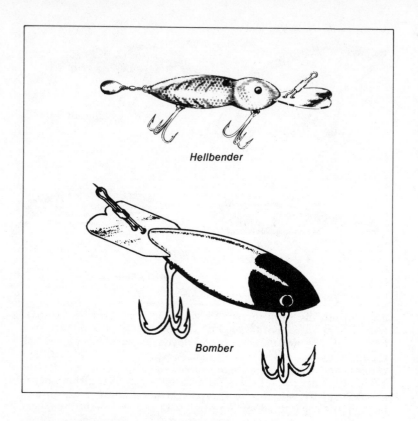

Hellbender

Bomber

DEEP-RUNNING CRANK BAITS

There are only two basic designs which can send a plug really deep—deep enough to plumb the bottom of a reservoir lake or reach productive depths over the outside reefs.

One design is that which features a very large lip.

The other is a combination design—a planing head of some sort, combined with additional weight inside the lure.

Weight alone is not enough to keep a plug running real deep on a troll or a fast retrieve. You can prove this quickly with a heavy lead jig. Though one of the best lures of all for deep-casting with a slow retrieve, even a jig weighing several ounces will rise far off the bottom when you crank it fast, or troll it.

As already hinted, some shallow-running lures are offered in special deep models with much larger lips.

The great majority of deep-running plugs is used by anglers in deep lakes, particularly reservoir lakes. But deep-divers also work beautifully in salt water. They can be counted on to take grouper and snapper over the reefs; tarpon and snook in deep channels; kingfish and other pelagic species offshore.

Deep-diving plugs used in the sea, I repeat, should be beefed-up models with heavy hooks, preferably wired through.

Sea Hawk

Bagley Divin' B

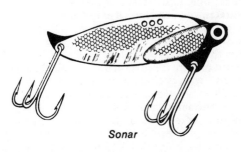

Sonar

Deep Rebel

PLASTIC WORMS AND EELS

Here's a subject which not only COULD fill a book of its own but SHOULD fill one. These baits, molded of soft plastic, come in every conceivable shade of color, and any length from two inches up to a foot or longer.

Though many worms are ready-rigged with one, two, or three hooks, most really avid worm users prefer to rig their own.

As for rigged worms, they work too, and they sell well enough. But worm specialists just like to rig their own.

Plastic worms have assumed a premier position in freshwater fishing, and recent saltwater developments have come along so fast, and in many specialties, that the worms seem destined to assume a like status among salty anglers.

Their use in salt water has thus far been primarily in combination with lead-head jigs. (See the section on "Jigs" for more detail.) However, new uses are being discovered every day. For instance, the plain, unleaded worm has taken tarpon, snook, grouper, snapper and numerous other species. In certain situations it produces nearly as well as natural bait. What situations? The field is so wide open all anglers should do their own experimenting.

Some of the newly-discovered uses of plastic worms are real eyebrow-raisers. Fishermen have used a simple worm on a popping-cork rig, instead of shrimp or other natural bait, and have made hefty catches of trout. Others have drifted worms behind a moving boat, both on the flats and in deeper water, and socked trout, jack, snapper, barracuda, and many other types.

What about color? In fresh water, standard colors for a long time have been black, blue and purple. However, many other hues are in wide use—green, various shades of red, spotted patterns, yellow, amber. Keep several colors on hand. Be guided by local advice, but don't be afraid to vary your colors if fishing is slow.

In salt water, the chief worm colors used so far have been yellow, white, pink—and orange for tarpon and snook. Also popular at sea is the clear worm, with a phosphorescent finish that glows in the dark. There isn't much light, you know, at depths of 100 feet or more, and the luminous worm does good work down there.

Though vast numbers of six-inch worms are still sold, the trend lately has been to bigger and bigger worms for bass fishing. Eight, nine and 10-inch lengths have come into their own. They seem to entice bigger bass without cutting down much, if any, on the number of strikes from smaller ones.

RIGGING THE WORM

The original self-rigged worm is shown in the first illustration— a single hook stuck into the worm at the head. This is still a good rig, particularly with six-inch worms and in open water. It can be used without a weight of any kind and allowed to settle slowly, or allowed to drift with the current—and adding a bit of rod action from time to time. If it must be sent deeper, you add a split shot, perhaps two, immediately in front of the hook. At least one shot is

Creme Scoundrel

Creme 2-hook, weedless

Bagley Tournament

Mann Jelly Worm

Springtail, rigged weedless

Creme Angle Worm, rigged

Boone Swirl Tail

generally used in a lake or other still water, so that the worm can go to bottom and be retrieved slowly, with a stop-and-go technique.

If weeds are a problem, or if the bottom is snaggy, the same rig can be effected by substituting a weedless hook for the plain hook.

Weedless hooks, though, have largely lost out in angler esteem to special "worm hooks," designed so that the worm itself serves as a weed guard. Worm hooks have an abrupt bend or angle in the shank, just behind the eye of the hook. They are rigged as shown in the third illustration—only the bent portion of the shank goes into the head of the worm. The rest of the hook stays outside, except for the point and barb, which is pushed up into the worm and left buried.

Weedless rigging can be accomplished in the same way with hooks of traditional pattern, via the "Texas Rig." The Sproat pattern is most widely used, although Aberdeen works well too. In the Texas Rig you insert the hook point into the head of the worm and bring it out only a quarter-inch or so below. Then the hook is spun completely around and pulled down so that the hook-eye is buried in the head of the worm. Last, the hook point is inserted into the body of the worm. Since there is no sharp bend on the shank to serve as an anchor, it is common practice to insert a round wooden toothpick through the worm and the hook-eye. The toothpick is then trimmed flush with the worm to anchor it.

Various specialty hooks are available for worm-rigging. A special Lew Childre hook has a point-and-barb instead of the conventional eye. This is simply inserted into the head of the worm. The regular hook point then is inserted into the worm in conventional fashion. A somewhat similar design is the Mister Twister hook, which does have a regular eye, but attached thereto is a small barbed shaft which is inserted into the worm head.

With the Texas rig, and most other worm rigs, care is taken to see that the worm lies as straight as possible on the hook to avoid twisting: however, some worm rigs are deliberately designed to spin or twist on the retrieve. At times, the spinning worm is definitely more productive. To rig a worm for spinning, you simply push the hook point farther down the worm on the original insertion—an inch or so—and leave a pronounced bend in the worm when the rig is finished. To help avoid line twist, a spinning worm should be used with a swivel, placed a foot or so above the worm.

Any worm rigged with the hookpoint buried should be used with quite a stiff rod. You have to take up all slack and give a mighty yank to make sure the point goes through the worm and into the fish. This is the reason stiff-action freshwater rods, either baitcasting or spinning, are so often referred to as "worm rods."

Also relatively new is a type of sliding sinker called a "worm lead" or "cone lead." Generally used in combination with the worm-hook rig, it is similar to the old familiar egg sinker, except that its pointed cone shape allows it to slither more easily through weeds or among snags.

Basic system for fishing a plastic worm, rigged or unrigged, is to let it sink to bottom and then jig it slowly back to you with short upward lifts of the rod tip, and pauses in between.

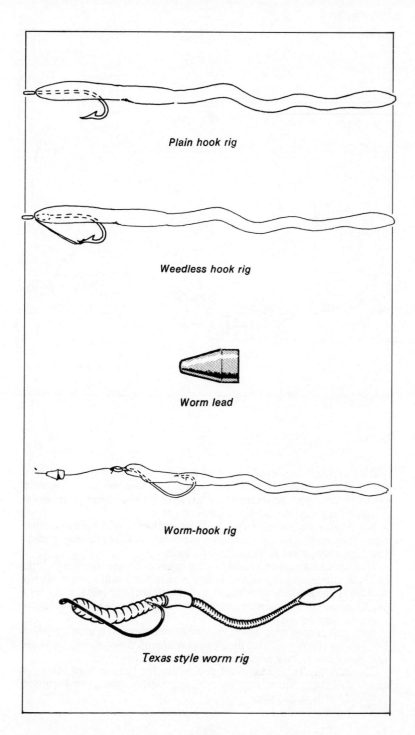

Plain hook rig

Weedless hook rig

Worm lead

Worm-hook rig

Texas style worm rig

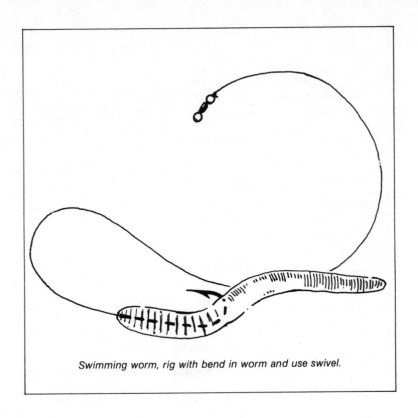

Swimming worm, rig with bend in worm and use swivel.

But, as with any other kind of fishing, the basic system is not enough. Sometimes the worm produces more strikes if wound steadily through the water at a slow speed. Other times, a medium or even fast retrieve is needed to attract fish.

Not a few fishermen use worms just as they would a plug or other lure. They cast it to the shoreline, retrieve a few feet in stop-and-go fashion, then wind it in and cast again.

The weedless-rigged worm is also a sensational lure for fishing in thick grass and lily pads. Toss it out in the jungle, wind slowly and let it snake around reeds or over the top of lily pads. If it hits a small pocket of open water, let it sink a few seconds before starting it on its way again.

As a rule, some drop-back, or slack line, should be given when a bass takes the worm. But don't wait too long. As soon as you sense fair pressure or any sort of steady pull—hit him.

There really is no standard procedure for timing your strike in worm fishing. When you gain some experience, your intuition probably will take over.

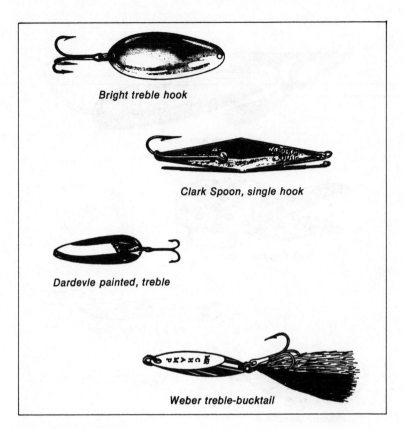

Bright treble hook

Clark Spoon, single hook

Dardevle painted, treble

Weber treble-bucktail

SPOONS

Spoons are one of the oldest and simplest types of artificial lure, yet still popular and productive everywhere—in salt water and fresh water.

Though you'll find many slight variations in shape and great variation in color and finish, all spoons work in essentially the same way—their dished-out shape giving them a wobbling or darting motion, and their metallic finish providing flash.

Spoons painted on one side and shiny on the other are frequently used in fresh water, but seldom in coastal fishing. In fact, the saltwater spoon fisherman is in pretty much of a rut. He may use spoons of different sizes and different designs, but he almost always insists on silver ones.

The freshwater man, on the other hand, may often use a painted spoon. He also will probably use silver under bright conditions; gold during an overcast; black on a very dark day or at night.

Treble-hooked spoons are used mostly for casting—either in open fresh waters, particularly for schooling fish, or in open salt water for such fish as mackerel, blues and trout.

185

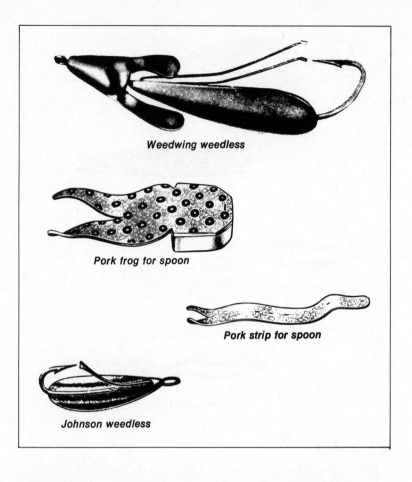

Weedwing weedless

Pork frog for spoon

Pork strip for spoon

Johnson weedless

The saltwater fisherman uses many more single-hook spoons than the inland angler, both for casting and trolling. However, a weedless spoon with a single hook is one of the ancient standbys in fresh water for fishing in thick grass, pads, or snaggy shallows.

The freshwater weedless spoon is almost always fitted with a trailer of some sort—a strip of pork rind, a pork-chunk frog, a plastic skirt or a plastic worm.

About 90 per cent of the time, a straight and fairly slow retrieve gives any spoon its best payoff punch. In thick weeds, though, it's a good idea to try holding your rod tip high, cranking fast, and making your spoon skitter along the top of the grass.

Believe it or not, bass can shoulder their way through all kinds of submerged moss and weeds and nail a fast-moving spoon on top of the water. If they do miss, you at least see where they are and can cast to the same spot and try a slower return.

See the chapter on "Saltwater Baits and Lures" for tips on trolling a spoon in salt water.

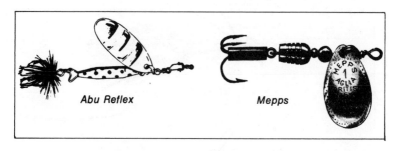

Abu Reflex

Mepps

SPINNERS AND SPINNER BAITS

The spinner is an ancient type of fishing lure and comes in many sizes, shapes and forms.

But when you hear the term "spinner bait," it refers to one branch of the spinner family which has boomed so much in recent years that it now is nearly as popular among bass anglers throughout the country as are plastic worms. In this type lure, the single or double spinner revolves *above* the dressed hook, as shown in the accompanying illustrations. The basic retrieve is a slow, steady one, but the spinner bait also is deadly when used much like a jig—with an up-and-down retrieve near bottom in deep water.

"Buzz baits" of which the best-known is the Lunker Lure, are spinner baits with large and modified spinners designed to remain on the surface, even at slow retrieves. This concept in fishing has proven very effective in varied water conditions, from deep impoundments to brush lakes and ponds. The Lunker Lures are almost weedless, due to the oversize spinner that "walks" over and around weed clumps.

Spinners are almost entirely used in fresh water, but for all types of freshwater fish from small bream and mountain trout to huge largemouth bass, pike and muskies. Many fish in salt water will take spinners, but the lure never has caught on well in the sea.

Manufactured spinner-type lures are numerous, among the best known ones being the Abu Reflex, Shyster, Toni and, of course, the various Mepps lures. Generally, they run from one-eighth to one-half ounce in weight. Larger ones are made.

The one-eighth and one-quarter ounce spinners get my vote as the best lure you can throw in fresh water—for sheer variety. I have caught hundreds of bream over the years with little spinners, and equal hundreds of small to medium bass. There are a lot of better lures for large bass, but the lunkers do hit tiny spinners occasionally. In addition to bass and bream, spinners *regularly* take pickerel, crappie (speckled perch), warmouth, northern species of perch, white bass, freshwater trout, and of course, rough fish such as gars and mudfish. In short, anything that feeds on either minnows or insect life is apt to slug a little spinner. I have even caught quite a few catfish on them.

Of course, there are larger spinners designed for larger fish. The Hawaiian Wigglers have been producing big bass for many years

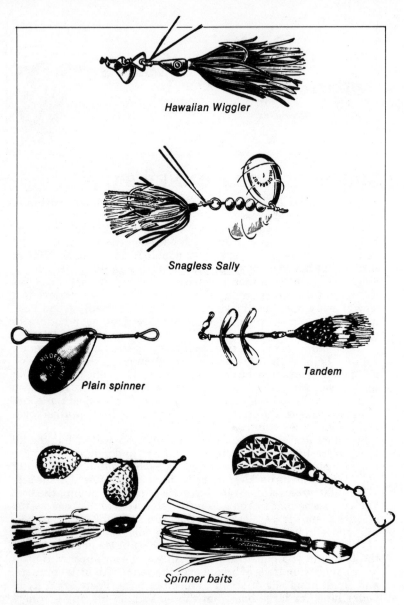

Hawaiian Wiggler

Snagless Sally

Plain spinner

Tandem

Spinner baits

under weedy and semi-weedy conditions. The Shimmy Wiggler has been around even longer, while one version or another of the Yellow Sally spinner is familiar to several generations of fishermen.

Then too, the fisherman has a huge choice of plain spinners with which to create his own lures. They come small enough to use ahead of trout flies; large enough for custom-made bass and musky lures.

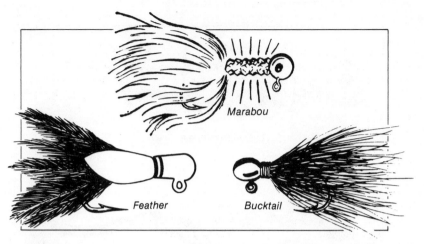

Marabou

Feather

Bucktail

JIGS

The word "jig" refers to a single hook, molded into a lead head and dressed with bucktail or other hairs, nylon filaments, feathers, Mylar strips, or any combination of those and similar materials.

It's possible that more anglers—in fresh and salt water combined—get more mileage out of jigs than any other type of artificial lure.

A new jig "material" has been added to the list of dressings in recent years—the plastic worm. Whether the worm is threaded onto the hook of a bare lead-head, or used as an added attraction with a bucktail jig, it does some pretty devastating work on a variety of fish, from inland waters to the deep sea.

Worm-jigs can be purchased in ready-made form, or can be fashioned in tailor-made style by the angler himself. The fisherman who makes his own can instantly create anything from a crappie or bonefish jig to an extra-heavy deep jig—just by threading a worm, or the tail piece of a worm, onto a lead-head of appropriate size.

A variety of other plastic tails also are used with jig heads, and the best of all probably is the curled, flattened tail which has the most natural swimming motion imaginable. A leading example of this type are the Creme lures called "Scally-Wag" (fresh water) and "Sea Scally" (salt water).

Plastic jig-tail styles that have achieved great popularity also include the Mann Grubs and Boone Touts, plus the Bagley Salty Dog and Salty Dog Shrimp.

Regardless of whether your jigs are dressed with conventional materials, plastic worms, or a combination of both, they are all fished in essentially the same style.

Most fish seem to prefer jigs when they are retrieved near bottom at a slow-to-medium speed. Crank the reel a few times, then twitch the rod to make the jig hop. Continue this pattern to boatside. But, as with all fishing rules, there are numerous exceptions. Fast retrieves sometimes produce better, particularly when going after

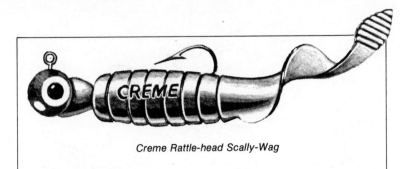

Creme Rattle-head Scally-Wag

Jig with Black Widow pork eel

mackerel or offshore species. And even the kinds of fish which normally prefer a slow, hopping retrieve can often be enticed out of a stubborn streak by changing suddenly from a slow retrieve to a fast one.

And when fishing lakes, you obviously would not hop your jig near bottom when fish are hitting at or near the surface.

How do you select the right jig? It really isn't too difficult a job, despite the hundreds of different jig designs and color variations.

The only consideration that might, of itself, spell success or failure is *weight*. Select weight according to your tackle and the depth you are trying to reach.

For freshwater fishing, and most inshore saltwater work—such as trout over flats, or for fishing along shorelines and around bars —the usual weight range is from one-eighth to one-half ounce.

Lighter weights will frequently prove useful for fish such as crappie or, in salt water, moonfish and other panfish. Of course, light weights cannot be used unless your tackle is light enough to toss them.

You'll need some jigs weighing five-eighths or one ounce, for deep-lake fishing; deep-hole coastal fishing; and for offshore and reef fishing in water up to say, 50 feet or so in depth. In water without current, a five-eighth or one-ounce jig can even be used at much greater depth.

Jigs larger than one-ounce in weight are used almost exclusively for deep-jigging offshore in water of around 80 to 150 feet. Such

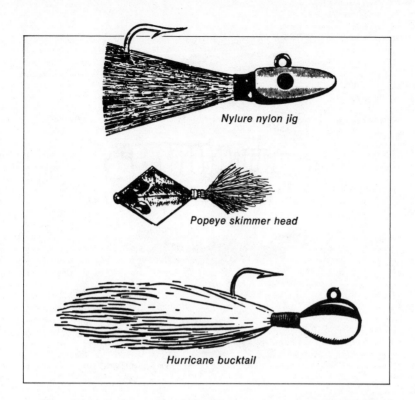

Nylure nylon jig

Popeye skimmer head

Hurricane bucktail

jigs may weigh two or three ounces. Big chunks of lead like that require extra-stout rods to even make them move at such depths.

Another factor in jig selection is *color,* but not so important as you might think. White and yellow have been standard colors for many years (both inland and in the sea), and you could probably get by very well on these alone. But there are many other popular hues—pink, orange, red, blue, brown and varied mixed patterns.

If you're just getting started, rely mostly on white and yellow. Experiment with a few others on the basis of local advice, and draw your own conclusions.

Now for the matter of dressing. Animal hairs and plastic worms seem to give the most lifelike actions, but feathers are not far behind. In fact, Marabou feathers are the wiggliest of all.

On the other hand, nylon is far more durable. A lot of fishermen use bucktail, feather or worm-jigs routinely, but keep nylon jigs handy for mackerel or other species which tear up jigs easily.

Note, however, that an awful lot of anglers use nylon jigs regularly for both freshwater and saltwater fish, and get consistently good catches. You can see, therefore, that choosing the proper dressing material is not exactly a critical thing.

Only one item of choice remains—head style. Here, except for a couple of specialized purposes, the choice matters hardly a bit.

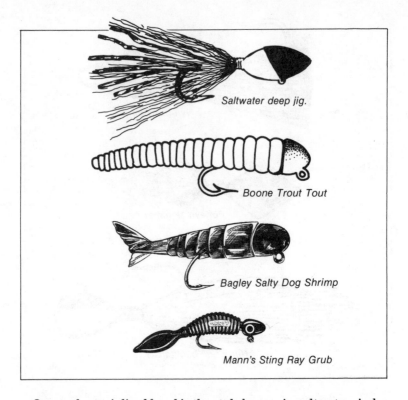

Saltwater deep jig.

Boone Trout Tout

Bagley Salty Dog Shrimp

Mann's Sting Ray Grub

One such specialized head is the style known in saltwater circles as a "skimmer," and in freshwater areas as a "glider." These have heads which are flattened horizontally, and sometimes slightly dished out. When retrieved, they plane upward in the water, hence the name "skimmer." They are preferred by bonefishermen, and other saltwater folks who fish very shallow flats.

Lake fishermen use the same type head for a different purpose. They allow it to sink slowly in deeper water. As it sinks it wobbles or "glides" with very enticing action—hence the other name, "glider."

Another specialty head is the deep-jigging head—flattened vertically rather than horizontally so that it offers less water resistance and sinks faster than jigs of the same weight, but with blunt or rounded heads.

For all-around use in shallow and medium depths, you'll find bullet-shaped heads, round heads, lima-bean-shaped heads, and others. Every style has its staunch followers and there is no way to determine which is "best."

Success with any jig, in any water, depends far more on how much you cast, and how much you experiment with retrievers, than it does on design, color or anything else.

Pick a weight that's suited to your tackle and water conditions, and you're in promising shape.

FLIES AND FLYROD LURES

It's hard to imagine, but there are many more variations in flies and flyrod lures than even in plugs or jigs or other kinds of artificials.

That's because for every one of the hundreds of different patterns and models offered by large suppliers, there are hundreds more variations made by small commercial tyers, or by individuals.

Many ponderous books have been written about fly patterns. We can only concern ourselves here with a look at the various categories of flies and flyrod lures, for familiarization.

Local advice is always of strong importance when selecting flies —particularly for freshwater trout fishing, but also for bass and panfishing, and saltwater fishing.

DRY FLIES—Dries are used in fresh water only, and can be identified by the very heavy hackling that allows them to float on the surface. Even so, they must be dressed to assure high floating qualities over extended periods. The dry fly user also false casts several times between actual casts to dry the fly. Dries are cast upcurrent, and must be allowed to float for as long a distance as possible without line drag.

In trout fishing, it is usually important to imitate—or at least strongly suggest—common insects of the particular locality when selecting dry fly patterns, especially if a "hatch" of insects is taking place.

Bream and other panfish take dry flies readily and often are not at all selective as to pattern.

WET FLIES are flies that do not float, but which are allowed to drift under the surface, usually near the top. Like dry flies, they are tied to imitate or suggest certain natural flies. Wets generally are cast across the current, or slightly upstream, and allowed a long, natural down-stream drift. The fisherman may strip line or twitch the rod-tip to provide extra action at the end of the drift.

Again, bluegills and other panfish take wet flies without much selectivity.

STREAMER FLIES are also fished "wet" but are made to imitate minnows instead of insects. Though they can often be drifted with good effect, they are usually stripped in with short jerks across current or down-current. In calm water, such as lakes or bays, streamers are always stripped in to imitate the erratic darting action of a small fish.

Almost all saltwater flies are streamers of large size.

Probably the most famous streamer of all these days is the Muddler—tied in a variety of sizes and deadly on all types of freshwater predatory fish from small trout to big bass.

Bass incidentally, are great streamer-fly fish. Bass streamers are mostly tied on hooks of No. 4 to No. 2/0 in size. Trout streamers generally are No. 10, 8, 6, sometimes smaller.

In the South, fly fishermen who go after bass use mostly popping bugs. Many who use popping bugs exclusively would be pleasantly

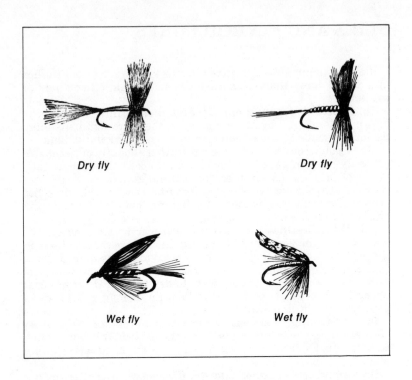

Dry fly

Dry fly

Wet fly

Wet fly

surprised indeed to see how streamers pay off many times when poppers aren't inducing any strikes at all.

NYMPHS are similar in usage to wet flies. However, they are tied to imitate the immature, or nymphal, stage of an insect rather than the adult, winged stage. Most nymphs are tied without wings, though there are tiny wings on some. Generally, they are tied for body conformation, perhaps with material to suggest legs.

Used almost entirely by trout fishermen, nymphs take panfish well in rivers and creeks. Local advice is vital in nymph selection.

MOLDED FLYROD LURES cover a wide range of actual molded imitations, in plastic, of nymphs, grubs, caterpillars, hellgramites, spiders, crickets, grasshoppers etc. A well-known example is the molded mayfly nymph so popular for bream and bass in southern waters. Trout anglers generally shun the molded imitations, but they are dear to the hearts of panfishermen everywhere.

FLYROD "HARD" LURES include tiny plugs, spoons and spinners, made much like their larger spinning-lure counterparts. They are not overly popular among fly fishermen—except for the little spinners, which often are used in combination with wet flies, or with natural bait, such as worms.

SALTWATER FLIES, as mentioned, are usually large streamers —tied either with animal hair, or with long feathers (hackle). A recent, and very good, trend has been to include a few strips of shiny Mylar in most all of the saltwater flies.

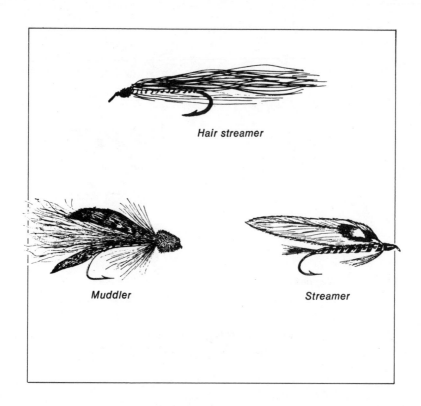

Hair streamer

Muddler

Streamer

You can seldom buy a good selection of saltwater flies, except in particular coastal areas where fly-fishing has become well-established. In such places, local tyers supply the stores.

Streamers for light saltwater use—small striped bass, snook, speckled trout, small tarpon, jack, ladyfish and other coastal varieties, should be about three inches in overall length, with a hook size of 2/0 or 3/0. Plain yellow, or plain white, in either hair or feather, are good producers. Mylar strips definitely help. There isn't a great deal of variation in pattern, but a wide choice in color combination. A streak of red, blue or black, helps in a white streamer. Red-and-yellow combinations are popular.

For all practical purposes, tarpon flies, offshore flies and other flies for big saltwater fish are merely enlarged versions of the coastal flies. They may have an overall length of up to six inches, and a hook up to 5/0 or 6/0, sometimes larger.

The most popular tarpon fly is a breathing feather streamer in yellow, orange, yellow-orange combination, or grizzly.

Perhaps the most popular offshore pattern is a big white fly tied with a dozen or more long hackles, and strips of Mylar.

As with freshwater fly fishing, it always pays to check for local preferences—though knowledgeable saltwater fly fishermen will be harder to find, even in areas where fly fishing is pretty popular.

Molded mayfly nymph

Molded cricket

Nymphs

Flyrod plug

Saltwater streamer

Multi-wing streamer

Bonefish fly

Bonefish shrimp fly

Rubber spider

POPPING BUGS

Popping Bugs are the flyrodder's equivalent of surface plugs. They float atop the water and are made to pop by twitching the rod upward. Only occasionally are they used by trout fishermen, but are standards for panfish and for bass. They are often used in saltwater too—in special ties, of course, with saltwater hooks.

Panfish poppers range from tiny things, as small as No. 10, to perhaps as large as No. 4. Bass poppers are usually found in the No. 4 to No. 2/0 size range, with Nos. 2, 1 and 1/0 being perhaps the most widely used. (Sizes refer to hook sizes.)

Popping bugs are made of cork, balsa, or hollow plastic, dressed with feather or hair "tails." A lot of them have rubber legs as well.

They should be fished slowly—popped, then allowed to rest. Faster retrieves may pay off at times.

Some bugs have bullet-shaped rather than popping heads. These are called "sliders" because they skim across the top without digging in and, of course, make less noise. They should be tried if the loud poppers don't work.

There are also hair bugs, made entirely of tightly-twisted or tied bucktail. These too ride the surface with little commotion and are deadly when fish seem spooky.

Another very popular type of floating "bug" is the sponge rubber spider with rubber legs—one of the best-liked of all bream lures.

197

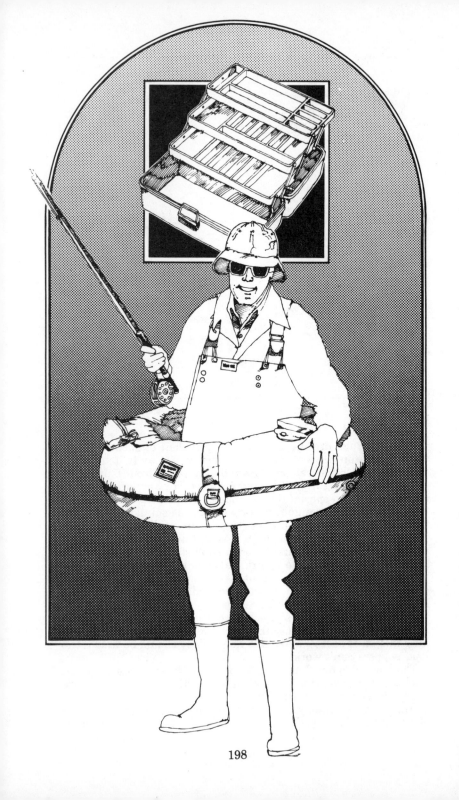

Chapter 5

Baits Rigs & Tackle

Fishing Accessories

Although the proper tackle, rigs and baits are at the heart of consistently successful fishing, the well-equipped angler relies on many accessory items as well. These range from such things as tackle boxes and bait containers—obvious and important fishing equipment—down to such supplies as insect repellent and fingernail clippers, which are easily overlooked or forgotten, but for which you would sometimes pay any price when you suddenly need them and don't have them on hand.

Some accessory gear is common to nearly all fishermen—nets, knives, coolers. Others must be chosen with particular types of angling in mind. A trout fisherman certainly doesn't need a flying gaff, and a tuna fisherman has little use for a fish stringer.

A wide range of accessories is described in this chapter, but there are many other useful items available to the angler. That's all to the good. It gives you a chance to spend additional hours browsing in your favorite tackle store or department.

ICE CHESTS OR COOLERS

A warm-weather fisherman's best friend is his cooler. One or more ice chests aboard a boat assures you of bringing home fish that are in peak table condition, and at the same time keeps a cooling drink close at hand when the sun is beating down.

Like tackle boxes, coolers come in a great variety of sizes, and even in several different styles. Though many of them can be considered pretty much "standard," there is still a lot of room for thoughtful choice in shopping.

For saltwater fishing, plastic chests are to be preferred, and freshwater anglers might prefer plastic too because of their generally light weight.

In making a selection, one good approach is to compromise on size and get the largest capacity which you can easily handle in transporting from home to car to boat. Certainly the most popular size range among fishermen is 40 to 50 quarts. Chests up to 60 quarts or so are marginal for one-man carrying, and larger coolers are two-man loads, but may be necessary if you're optimistic about getting many fish, or very large ones.

Medium or large coolers may well serve the average angler as repository for both his catch and his water and drinks. Mixing fish with drinks will require that you carefully clean the bottle before you drink, but that's a small price to pay for convenience.

On the other hand, if you have plenty of room, a large box for the catch (or the bait and the catch) plus a smaller one for drinks and lunch is a welcome combination.

There is no better way to handle your fish than to deposit them directly on ice. Even stringers do not preserve freshness nearly so well. Keep the whole fish on ice until you clean them. After cleaning, fish should be placed in plastic bags or other water-tight containers before going back into the cooler. Dressed fish should not be allowed to come into contact with water, even that which has recently melted from ice.

Though most modern ice chests are very good, there is some variation in cold-keeping ability. One ingenious method of increasing the life of ice is found in the Gott line of coolers, some of which have flat plastic bottles which are fastened to the inside of the lid. When filled with water and frozen, the bottles provide all the cold needed for pre-chilled items or for very short outings. When ice is in the box, they extend its thawing time greatly. The lid location of the bottles is the secret. If simply placed in the bottom of the box they would be inefficient, since hot air rises and cold settles.

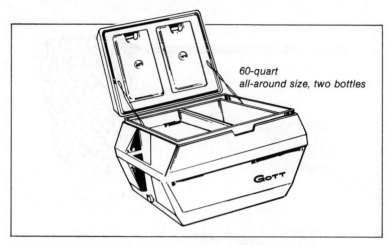

60-quart
all-around size, two bottles

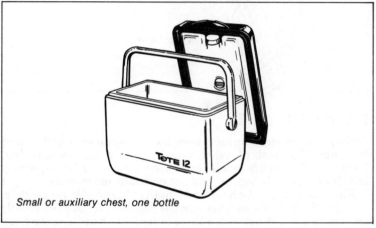

Small or auxiliary chest, one bottle

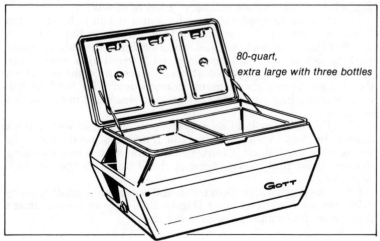

80-quart,
extra large with three bottles

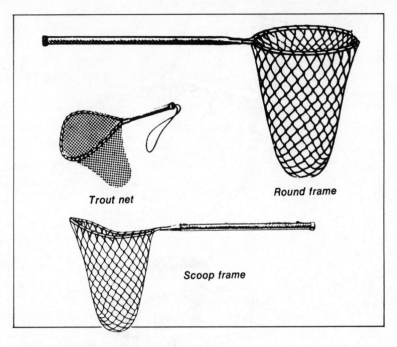

Trout net

Round frame

Scoop frame

LANDING NET

Most present-day landing nets have aluminum handles and framing, with mesh of nylon, plastic or, in some cases, rubber. Cotton mesh nets are available, but will weaken or rot, especially in saltwater use. Nylon nets do not cost that much more.

While diameter of the hoop and length of the handle vary widely, it's a good idea to use as large a net as you can comfortably handle and easily stow. A net with a three-to-four-foot handle, and a hoop diameter of 18-24 inches will serve most purposes.

Special long-handled nets can be found if you fish, say, from docks or seawalls. But for fishing from structures higher than a few feet (many ocean piers and many bridges), the only practical landing net to use is a large hoop net lowered by a rope. These specialized nets are provided at many piers and some fishermen carry them to bridges. A more common device for landing fish from bridges, however, is the *bridge gaff,* described in the section on gaffs.

With the ordinary landing net, scoop up your fish with a quick motion, but not a wild splashing one. If possible, put the net in the water, lead the fish close to it, and net him with a fast sweeping motion, head first. If you touch a fish's tail with the net, he'll scoot away.

Check nets often for rips or tears, and repair even small holes by tying the mesh with nylon or Dacron line, or even monofilament line. Small holes quickly become big ones.

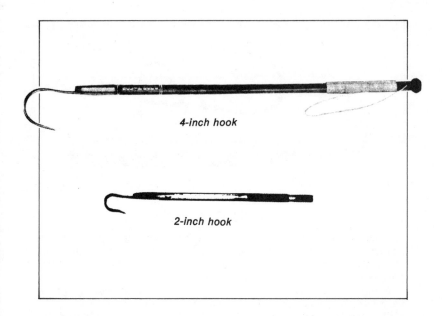

4-inch hook

2-inch hook

GAFFS

Although a net serves most landing needs for the freshwater and inshore saltwater fisherman, anyone who fishes the reefs or offshore waters should definitely have a gaff aboard. Even inshore you're likely to need a gaff from time to time in order to handle a catch too large to get in your net. Should such a happy occasion arise, you'll be very glad indeed you have a gaff.

Best all-around gaff for light use is one with a stainless steel, two-inch hook—that is, the distance from point straight across to shaft is two inches. A three or four-foot handle is long enough for most small boats. For boats with high transoms, a six or eight-foot handle may be needed.

The two-inch hook is preferred for small-game fishing because it can be difficult to stick a fish like a school king mackerel or school dolphin with a larger hook. At the same time, however, the two-incher is satisfactory for much larger catches.

If you do a lot of offshore fishing though, it would be wise to complement the two-inch gaff with another, larger one—say a four-inch.

To use a gaff, lower the hook into the water under the fish, then tug smoothly upward to drive the point home. The fish should be hoisted up and into the boat with as little interruption of motion as you can manage, for many fish are adept at tearing loose from a gaff.

Specialty gaffs are made for a variety of purposes, and can be highly useful, or downright essential, depending on your own fishing activities. Let's look at some of them:

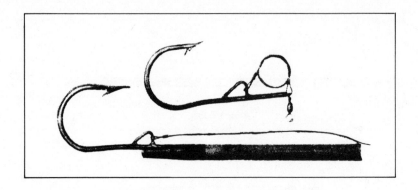

FLYING GAFF

Used mostly by big-game fishermen, but occasionally by inshore anglers who go after jewfish, say, or sharks, the flying gaff features a separate handle and hook. These are fitted together with a temporary fastening, usually light line.

When the gaff hook is driven into a fish, the temporary tie gives way and the hook comes loose from the handle.

Of course, there is a stout rope tied to an eye in the hook, and the other end of the rope is secured firmly to a cleat on the boat.

Once a fish is on the flying gaff, the handle is set aside.

The point of the flying gaff is flattened, sharpened and barbed —all the better to penetrate the tough hide of a big fish, and to resist pulling out once it has been buried.

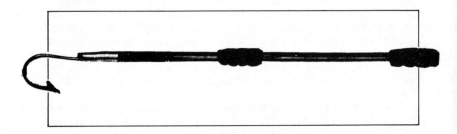

TARPON GAFF

An ordinary gaff can be used on tarpon in the small-to-medium weight ranges. But guides and fishermen who go after giant tarpon, and who want them in the boat, will rig a special tarpon gaff.

This is a large gaff hook—at least six inches. And, like a flying gaff hook, it is flattened at the point, barbed, and sharpened to a knife-edge. The hook is mounted firmly on a stout six-to-eight foot handle.

A true flying gaff is considered too hazardous for use on big tarpon from small boats.

When gaffing a big tarpon, try to hit him near the mid-section, rather than at the "shoulders" or tail.

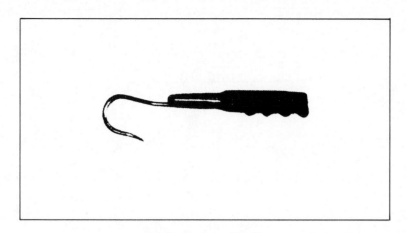

RELEASE GAFF

A release gaff is nothing more than a small gaff hook with a very short handle—just large enough to hold in one hand. Some release gaffs have no handle at all—just a loop of rope which is slipped around the gaffer's wrist. The loop, of course, must be large enough so that you can slip out of it instantly if the situation requires.

The release gaff is used mainly on tarpon (of all sizes) which you want to release, while doing the fish as little harm as possible.

Play the fish until he is *thoroughly* whipped. Once he is beside the boat and inactive, you slip the small gaff hook into his mouth, and bring the point through his lower jaw. Now you can hold him while you remove the hook, or cut the leader.

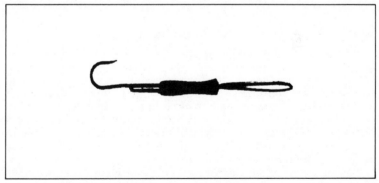

SURF GAFF OR "PICK"

The surf gaff is identical to the release gaff, except that it might have a larger hook. It is worn at the belt by surf fishermen. When they hook and whip a large fish, such as a channel bass or striped bass, they gaff him around the head or "shoulders," and use the short-handled gaff to drag him up the beach.

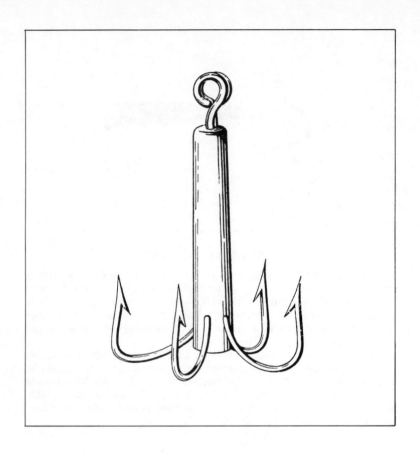

BRIDGE GAFF

The bridge gaff is really a large gang hook (usually a 10/0 size) which has a hefty chunk of lead molded around the hook shanks.

Since many bridges are too high to permit use of a conventional gaff with a conventional handle, the bridge gaff is used because it works well and can be easily stowed in a bridge-fisherman's kit.

The bridge gaff is tied to a stout line, usually nylon cord. After a fish is whipped and lying on its side below, the fisherman snaps an ordinary shower-curtain ring around both his fishing line and the gaff cord. Then he lowers the gaff.

The shower-curtain ring serves as a guide to steer the gaff to the fish's head. And the ring is large enough so that it can slip over any swivel or other terminal tackle on the fishing line.

The angler may have to do a bit of jiggling with either or both lines to make sure the gaff slides all the way into position.

Once the gang hook is at the fish's head, the angler jerks the cord until the hook takes hold, then handlines his fish up to the catwalk.

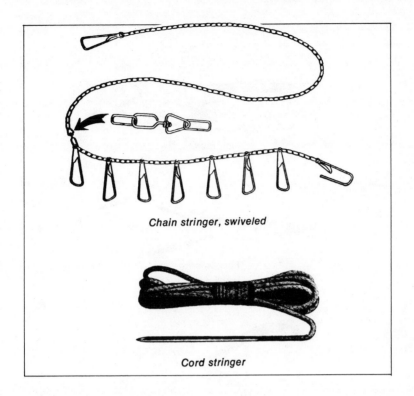

Chain stringer, swiveled

Cord stringer

FISH STRINGERS

The two common types of fish stringers are the ordinary cord stringer, and the chain stringer with individual fish clips.

Made of cotton, nylon or twisted plastic, the cord stringer is fitted with a metal point at one end; a metal ring at the other. This type is used principally for panfish, but can be used for larger fish as well. You run the point under the fish's gill cover and out its mouth. Then you run the point through the metal ring. With all the fish after the first, you simply run the point in the gill and out the mouth, sliding the fish to the bottom of the string.

The chain stringers feature safety-pin type clips, usually of spring metal wire, but sometimes of nylon. Favored by bass fishermen, this type stringer is used by opening the "safety pin" and running the point through both lips of the fish. The pin is then snapped shut.

Cord stringers can be obtained in various lengths. The usual is six feet, for use when fishing from a skiff or from shore. Longer ones may be needed by bridge or dock fishermen.

Most freshwater fish and some saltwater species will stay alive for hours if kept on a stringer in the water—that is, if they are not injured beforehand.

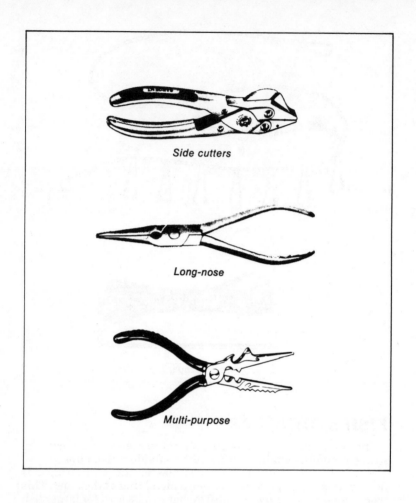

Side cutters

Long-nose

Multi-purpose

FISHERMAN'S PLIERS

Wire-cutting pliers are just about a must for saltwater fishermen, and not much less useful to the freshwater fan—because they clip monofilament line and leader, as well as wire.

You have your choice of two basic styles. One is the blunt-nosed, square-jaw type with the cutters on the outside. With this style, you can cut wire much easier and faster.

The other is the long-nose type, with the cutters at the base of the jaws. This kind is somewhat more unhandy when it comes to clipping wire, but it does clip efficiently—and its long jaws are often a big help in removing hooks from a fish's gullet.

There are also some long-nosed pliers which feature additional accessories—such as a bottle opener, or perhaps even an adjustable wrench in the handle.

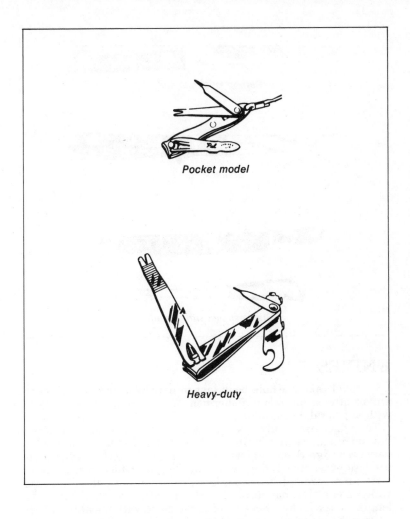

Pocket model

Heavy-duty

FINGERNAIL CLIPPERS

The familiar pair of fingernail clippers is one of the handiest gadgets an angler can use. No tool is better for clipping line.

Some brands of this type clipper are designed especially for fishermen, and may feature additional accessories—such as a cord for looping to a buttonhole, and a blunted needle for clearing hook-eyes or picking out tangles.

However, the accessories aren't used nearly so often as the clippers themselves, and so for all practical purposes the ordinary fingernail clippers from the drug counter do just as well.

CAUTION: Never attempt to clip wire of any kind with fingernail clippers. You'll only blunt the edges and ruin them.

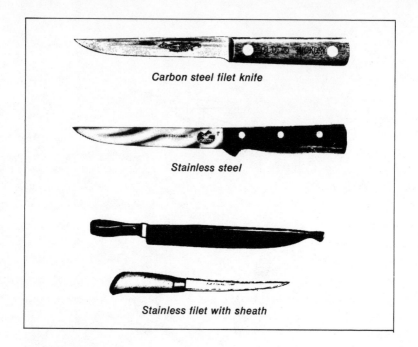

Carbon steel filet knife

Stainless steel

Stainless filet with sheath

KNIVES

It would take a whole book just to list the different models of knives offered for sale to fishermen. We'll content ourselves here with a general discussion.

Though it hasn't always been so, you can now get numerous brands of knives with stainless steel blades that take and hold a very keen edge. Some anglers still prefer carbon steel knives, which are less expensive and easy to sharpen, but which rust quickly.

As an all-around fisherman's knife, I nominate the fillet-type which has a thin but sturdy blade of stainless steel, and a blade length of six inches. Several of these come with sheaths, which protect the blade when stowed in a tackle box, and which can be worn at your belt while fishing.

Such a knife does a great job of filleting fish, cutting bait, or making rigged baits.

The stainless steel blade has this additional advantage: It can be cleaned up spick and span in a minute, and used for preparing your lunch!

Panfishermen, though, might find the six-inch blade too large for convenient dressing of a mess of bream. Best knife for this job is a good sharp pocket knife.

The various "gadget" knives for fishermen—such as folding knives with bottle-openers, scaling edges, etc.—should be selected by the individual for whatever appeal or value they might have to him.

HONE OR FILE

Every angler's tackle box should contain a sharpening tool—both for his knife and for his hooks.

A small whetstone will do a pretty good job of both. But it isn't a bad idea to carry a larger stone for the knife (it's faster and easier), and either a small stone or a small file for putting a keen point on hooks.

With light-wire freshwater hooks it may be easier, and not expensive, to change hooks when the point gets dull or blunted.

The majority of saltwater hooks, even new ones, can do with a bit of sharpening. Being thicker, these hooks are harder to set in a fish. Just a lick or two with hone or file might well save you a trophy fish.

LUBRICANTS

Always carry oil with you when fishing. The level wind mechanism of a revolving spool casting reel should be oiled once or twice during a fishing day for peak performance. And it never hurts, either to drop a bit of oil on both moving ends of a spinning reel bail sometime during the day.

Heavier grease is seldom necessary during an actual fishing trip —since this type lubricant is used mainly inside a reel on the gears.

By far the most useful and versatile of lubricants are the sprays which come in aerosol cans. I strongly recommend carrying a can in the tackle box. If you have a small box, you can buy a small can, but the larger sizes are more economical.

Spray the stuff lightly over all of your reels. It lubricates the external moving parts mentioned above, and also protects your reel from salt spray. The stuff doesn't harm your fishing line.

Don't hesitate to spray *anything* you wish to protect from corrosion or exposure to salt—rods, reel seats, tackle box hinges, boat hardware, battery terminals, zippers, outboard motors.

These sprays displace moisture and improve electrical contacts, in addition to fighting corrosion.

Be sure to spray your reels, reel seats and rod guides after fishing. Also spray hooks and lures before returning them to your tackle box.

INSECT REPELLENTS

An item often overlooked by an angler—and sometimes to his great pain and suffering—is insect repellent.

If you can't spare the space in your tackle box for a spray-can, you can at least carry a small bottle of repellent lotion, or a stick.

I'd hate to try remembering the times I've been caught without repellent because I didn't think the mosquitoes would be troublesome at that particular place or that particular season.

If you do get caught without repellent and the bugs begin to attack, rub your exposed skin lightly with motor oil—a bit messy, but it works. If you don't have any motor oil, run!

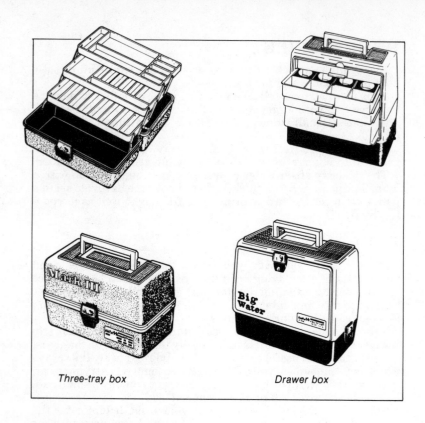

Three-tray box   *Drawer box*

TACKLE BOXES

Tackle boxes come in an endless array of sizes, shapes, makeups and material.

Every angler must select his own to fill his particular needs. Here are some general observations:

Plastic boxes are by far the best for saltwater use. Wooden boxes are good, but expensive and heavy.

Aluminum boxes are excellent for freshwater fishermen because they are both strong and light.

If you fish often from small boats where space is at a premium, you might consider getting two small tackle boxes rather than a single large one. Big boxes can be difficult to open in limited space.

Get some small divided boxes of clear plastic. They can be used to sort small items inside a larger box, and also serve as pocket tackle boxes when you wade or bank-fish.

Plastic dividers in most new tackle boxes are resistant to the corrosive effects of plastic worms. Some of the older plastics are not. In any event, it's a good idea to get one or more "worm boxes" —special small plastic boxes with long compartments—which are not harmed by contact with plastic worms. Carry these inside your regular tackle box.

Satchel type box

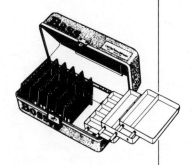

Spinnerbait box

Hip-roof, six-tray box

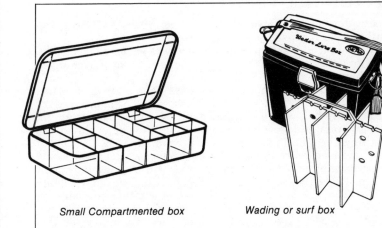

Small Compartmented box

Wading or surf box

COTTON GLOVES

Heavy-duty cotton gloves are vital when fishing offshore; frequently useful for inshore fishing as well.

Always wear gloves when handling a wire leader as you lead a fish in for gaffing. Even if the leader is monofilament, gloves might save a burn.

Caution dictates you should wear gloves when gaffing a fish too, although many experienced fishermen do not. The same goes for handling any fish with teeth, sharp gills or dorsal spines. Again, many experienced folks don't take the trouble to put on gloves. It's something like ignoring the seat belt in your car—999 times out of 1000 there's no harm done. But that thousandth time—oh boy!

A great many private boaters now seek sailfish, and they often get them. Gloves are essential for proper boating, or even releasing, of a sail. You should not use a gaff, but should take the leader in gloved hands and carefully pull the sail close enough so you can get both gloved hands around his bill. Then you either pull him aboard and clobber him, or else cut the leader and let him go.

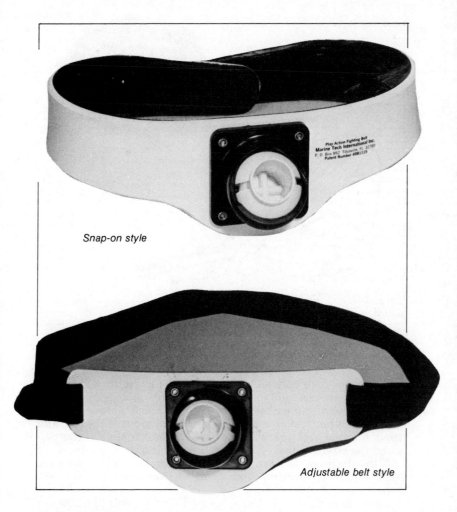

Snap-on style

Adjustable belt style

ROD BELT

In saltwater fishing you may be called upon to fight a fish for many minutes, an hour, maybe two hours or more. Unless you have a rod belt with a socket in which to rest the rod butt, you'll end up with a very sore tummy indeed.

This goes for light, one-hand tackle as well as for a heavy ocean rod.

If you do not use rods with gimbal butts, you'll need only a leather rod belt with leather cup or socket.

For gimbal butts, you need a gimbal belt—that is, a deep socket fitted with a pin, and usually on a swiveling or semi-swiveling mount. The pin, of course, fits into the gimbal slot of your rod butt, and helps you keep the rod upright as you do battle.

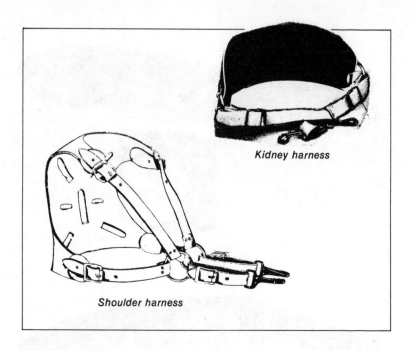

Kidney harness

Shoulder harness

ROD HARNESSES

Harnesses help considerably during long fights with ocean tackle, and are essential for big-game fishing—marlin, giant tuna, deep-fighting of big amberjack or grouper, shark fishing.

Without a harness, you must support the weight of the rod, and apply fighting pressure, with your arms alone. Nobody's arms can stand the strain of this, except with light classes of tackle.

With a harness, you can let your shoulders or back do the hard work, and can even drop your arms to your sides for brief rest periods.

One type of harness is the *shoulder harness,* made of leather or of heavy canvas with leather straps. You put this on as you would a vest. Two straps in front of you are clipped to the harness rings of your ocean reel. The rod butt, of course, rests either in your gimbal belt, if standing, or in the gimbal of your fishing chair, if seated.

The other type of harness is the *kidney harness,* which is always used in conjunction with a fighting chair—never by an angler who is standing.

The kidney harness is nothing more than a very strong and heavily padded belt which fits around your lower back. The ends of this belt, in front, are connected to the reel rings by means of heavy ropes or straps and metal snaps.

Usually the kidney harness is made with an integral padded seat, on which the angler sits. This is useful because it keeps the harness from "riding up" the angler's back while he's fighting the fish.

Fisherman's model glasses and handy clip-on style

POLARIZING SUNGLASSES

Any good sunglass contributes to your comfort while fishing, but only those with polarizing lenses cut out enough glare to allow you to see much under the surface of the water.

Without polarizing glasses, the bonefisherman might as well stay home. Many other fish are also hunted by sight on the flats, and polarizing glasses are equally essential for all of them.

Even if you don't fish the flats, you would do well to wear polarizing glasses as a matter of routine. In any kind of water, fresh or salt, they'll improve your vision in regard to such things as picking out underwater limbs; distinguishing the wakes of fish from wind ripples; or studying the bottom conditions in reasonably shallow water.

You also might see a lot of fish in fairly deep water that you might miss if not wearing the glasses.

In case you are confused by terminology, the words "Polaroid" and "polarizing" mean essentially the same thing. "Polaroid" is a brand name and is capitalized. "Polarizing" is a generic term, used for all glasses of this type.

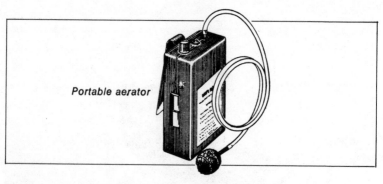

Portable aerator

BAIT BUCKETS AND BOXES

The simplest bait buckets are merely containers which hold water, and which have lids to keep the bait from jumping out. But to hold bait for any length of time, or in any quantity, provisions must be made to replenish the available oxygen supply in the water.

Buckets made of papier-mache or plastic foam hold the oxygen supply better and longer than metal or solid plastic buckets.

To assure an oxygen supply in any container, however, you should take one or more of the following steps:

1. Use O-Tabs, a commercial product which releases oxygen into the water.

2. Change water at frequent intervals, if possible.

3. Keep water cool and shaded. Adding chunks of ice can help.

4. Best of all, use a small pump or aerator. Some very good ones are available at low cost. They clip to the side of the bucket and run on flashlight batteries. For big bait containers, there are heavy-duty aerators which connect to the battery of a boat.

* * *

Two-piece buckets are popular. These have an inner, perforated container, in which the bait is kept. The inner container is removed and held in the water on a heavy cord. To transport bait, you simply fill the outer bucket with water and place the inner container into it.

There are one-piece buckets which do a similar job. These hold enough water in the bottom to transport bait. But they have perforations at the top, so that when the bucket is lowered by cord from boat or bridge, water freely circulates and keeps the bait frisky.

Some live baits, of course, do not require water at all. Crickets and grasshoppers are kept in light cages of wire or plastic mesh. Some are bucket-shaped with a handle for carrying. Others are tube-shaped and can be worn at the belt.

Belt boxes also are available for carrying worms, grubs, sand maggots, etc.

Refer to the section on Live Shrimp in Chapter 4 for instructions on how to keep shrimp alive without water.

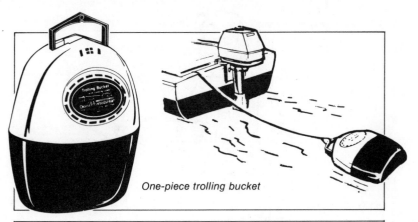

One-piece trolling bucket

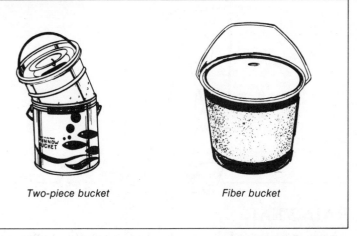

Two-piece bucket   *Fiber bucket*

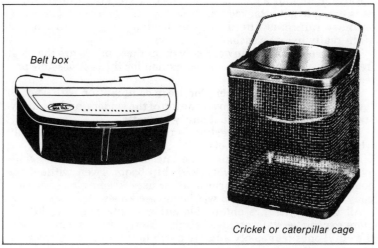

Belt box

Cricket or caterpillar cage

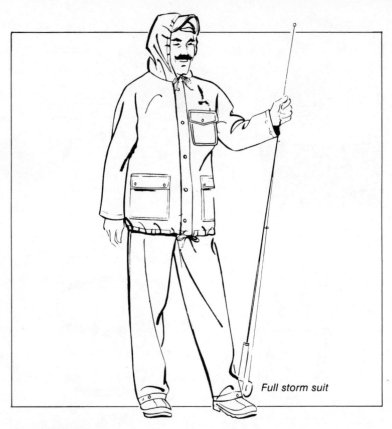

Full storm suit

RAINWEAR

Early in anyone's fishing career, he discovers two things—first, he is going to get attacked regularly by rain, spray or fog; second, ordinary raincoats afford little protection, and next to none at all in really heavy weather.

The three types of rainwear shown on these pages are the most frequently chosen by active outdoorsmen for the best possible protection from the elements.

The short parka is excellent for use in combination with waders. It extends below the waist, over the top of the waders, and the drawstring can be tighted against chilly updrafts.

The most complete protection is the full storm suit, especially when worn atop rubber boots.

An excellent compromise is the knee-length parka. This gives overall protection when worn with hip boots. Even without the boots it is adequate for warm-weather use—keeping most of your body dry, although you get wet below the knees.

All three styles are obtainable either in inexpensive vinyl or more expensive waterproofed fabric. Though welcome in a pinch, the vinyl ones tear easily and are much hotter to wear. Good raingear is worth its price.

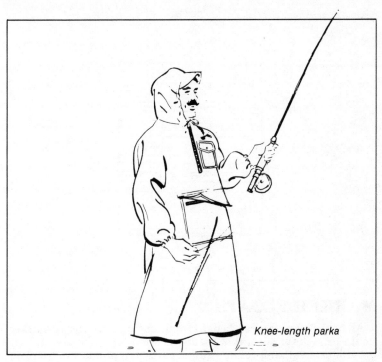

Knee-length parka

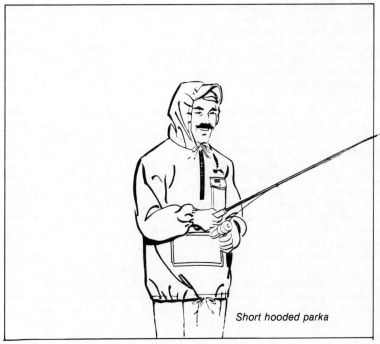

Short hooded parka

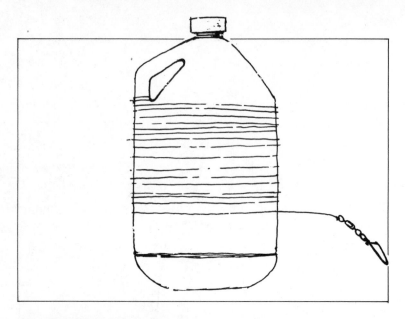

MARKER FLOATS

All boating anglers can benefit from keeping a pre-rigged marker float—or perhaps several of them—at hand for quick use. A float is extremely valuable for marking a particular productive spot you might locate, or for orientation in drift-fishing. You may drift for long periods with little or no luck, then suddenly start hitting some fish. Throw over the marker, and you will then be able to circle updrift of it and go back over the productive area repeatedly. It can be surprisingly difficult to retrace your same drifting course without such a marker, because a boat seldom drifts directly downwind, as it might seem—particularly in salt water, where currents may be involved.

In smooth, shallow water, your marker need be nothing more than a regular fishing float with light line and light sinker. The choppier the surface and the deeper the water, the larger your marker should be for visibility. A good choice for coastal fishing is a half-gallon bleach jug. Tie some discarded fishing line to the jug's grip, and wrap enough of the line around the jug to reach bottom in your fishing area—with an ample amount of extra line, or "scope" allowed. A large snap at the end of the line will allow you to affix a heavy sinker, or a piece of scrap metal of suitable weight, to the line. When you want to mark a spot, just toss over the jug. The sinking weight will spin the jug and unwrap the line automatically. When stowage space is a problem, and visibility not so bad, you can use a one-quart plastic bottle instead of the jug.

Lake fishermen can make excellent use of a series of small floats —either plastic bottles or fishing bobbers—for marking contours on the lake bottom, such as the course of an old stream bed, or a submerged point or long ledge.

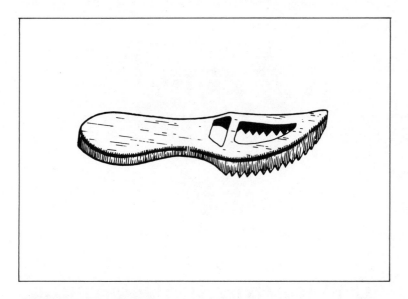

FISH SCALERS

With many species of fish, scaling presents no problem at all. The scales are small, soft and can be flicked away with light pressure of a pocket knife, or even a table knife.

Most members of the sunfish family—bluegills and crappie, for instance—are easily scaled. One especially nifty scaling device for those and other soft-scaled varieties is simply a garden hose. Use a restricting nozzle, turn the pressure up full and direct the flow of water "against the grain" while you hold a fish in your hand. If you have a big string of panfish to scale, the hose works wonders.

Saltwater fish are extremely variable in their willingness to give up their scales. A few, such as weakfish, are as quickly scaled as most freshwater fish. Others, such as red drum, are very tough. In general, saltwater varieties require more scaling effort, and you should *not* use a knife, because there's a strong chance the blade will slip, or will catch and skid, and give you a nasty cut. Simple scaling devices, of which one of many is pictured here, should be employed for heavy work. In a pinch, with no scaler handy, use the edge of a tablespoon.

You may, of course, wish to skin your fish rather than scale them. This is largely a matter of personal preference and experience with various kinds of fish. Many fish are much better when scaled and prepared with the skin left on. A few should always be skinned because the skin contains a "muddy" flavor. This is true of largemouth bass taken from most still, murky waters. While panfish generally are their sweetest when scaled, very large panfish taken from mud-bottomed lakes can definitely be improved by skinning.

Let Vic's Expertise Help You...

For more than 30 years, Vic Dunaway's by-line has been known to anglers all over the country, and in foreign lands as well. He has written hundreds of articles for national and regional magazines, and thousands of newspaper columns. He is, of course, a book author and also has appeared on four different television networks, as well as numerous local and syndicated programs.

Though skilled in many different angling specialties, and many writing styles, his strongest interest is in the teaching of fishing skills and enjoyment. Perhaps no other fishing writer has his knack for selecting just the right information on a particular angling subject and presenting it in the quickest, clearest manner—without unnecessary frills or padding.

In recent years, Dunaway has been editor of the award-winning *Florida Sportsman* Magazine and of the *Florida Sportsman Fishing Charts,* aimed at giving detailed where-to-go information for every section of the rambling Florida coast.

WICKSTROM
PUBLISHERS, INCORPORATED
5901 S.W. 74 STREET, MIAMI, FLORIDA 33143